MODERN WORLD HISTORY

Guided Reading Workbook

Contents

The Colonies Become New Nations

Struggles for Democracy

Global Interdependence

HOW TO USE THIS BOOK

The purpose of this *Guided Reading Workbook* is to help you read and understand your history textbook, *Modern World History.* You can use this *Guided Reading Workbook* in two ways.

1. **Use the *Guided Reading Workbook* side-by-side with the lessons in *Modern World History*.**

- Refer to the *Guided Reading Workbook* while you are reading each lesson in *Modern World History*. All of the heads in the *Guided Reading Workbook* match the heads in the lessons.

- Use the *Guided Reading Workbook* to help you read and organize the information in each lesson.

2. **Use the *Guided Reading Workbook* to study the material that will appear in the lesson tests.**

- Reread the summary of every lesson.

- Review the definitions of the **Key Terms and People** in the *Guided Reading Workbook*.

- Review the graphic organizer that you created as you read the summaries.

- Review your answers to questions.

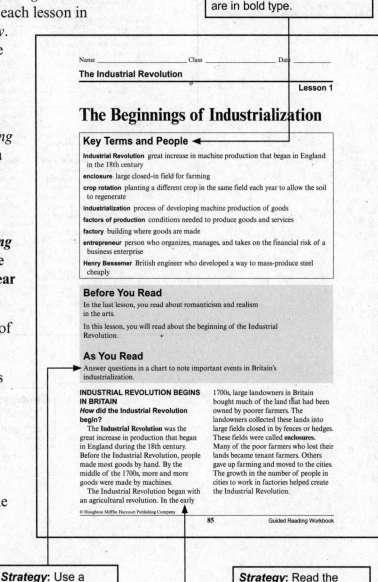

Strategy: Read the **Key Terms and People** and the definition of each. The **Key Terms and People** are in bold type.

Name _____ Class _____ Date _____
The Industrial Revolution

Lesson 1

The Beginnings of Industrialization

Key Terms and People

Industrial Revolution great increase in machine production that began in England in the 18th century

enclosure large closed-in field for farming

crop rotation planting a different crop in the same field each year to allow the soil to regenerate

industrialization process of developing machine production of goods

factors of production conditions needed to produce goods and services

factory building where goods are made

entrepreneur person who organizes, manages, and takes on the financial risk of a business enterprise

Henry Bessemer British engineer who developed a way to mass-produce steel cheaply

Before You Read

In the last lesson, you read about romanticism and realism in the arts.

In this lesson, you will read about the beginning of the Industrial Revolution.

As You Read

Answer questions in a chart to note important events in Britain's industrialization.

INDUSTRIAL REVOLUTION BEGINS IN BRITAIN
How did the Industrial Revolution begin?

The **Industrial Revolution** was the great increase in production that began in England during the 18th century. Before the Industrial Revolution, people made most goods by hand. By the middle of the 1700s, more and more goods were made by machines.

The Industrial Revolution began with an agricultural revolution. In the early 1700s, large landowners in Britain bought much of the land that had been owned by poorer farmers. The landowners collected these lands into large fields closed in by fences or hedges. These fields were called **enclosures.** Many of the poor farmers who lost their lands became tenant farmers. Others gave up farming and moved to the cities. The growth in the number of people in cities to work in factories helped create the Industrial Revolution.

© Houghton Mifflin Harcourt Publishing Company

85   Guided Reading Workbook

Strategy: Use a graphic organizer to help you organize information in the lesson.

Strategy: Read the summary. It contains the main ideas and the key information under the head.

Strategy: Underline the main ideas and key information as you read.

Lesson 1, *continued*

New farm methods made farmers more productive. For example, Jethro Tull invented a seed drill that made planting more efficient. Farmers also practiced **crop rotation**. Crop rotation is the practice of planting a different crop in the same field each year. This improves the quality of the soil.

Industrialization is the process of developing machine production of goods. For several reasons, Britain was the first country to industrialize. <u>Great Britain had all the resources needed for industrialization. These resources included coal, water, iron ore, rivers, harbors, and banks.</u> Britain also had all the **factors of production** that the Industrial Revolution required. These factors of production included land, labor (workers), and capital (wealth).

1. Why was Britain the first country to industrialize?

   _____

   _____

INVENTIONS SPUR INDUSTRIALIZATION
***What* inventions helped change business?**

The Industrial Revolution began in the textile industry. Several new inventions helped businesses make cloth and clothing more quickly. Richard Arkwright invented the water frame in 1769. It used water power to run spinning machines that made yarn. In 1779, Samuel Compton invented the spinning mule, which made better thread. In 1787, Edmund Cartwright developed the power loom. The power loom was a machine that sped up the cloth-making process.

These new inventions were large and expensive machines. They needed large **factories** to house and run these machines. **Entrepreneurs**, or people who start and manage businesses, built the factories near rivers because these machines ran on water power.

2. How was the textile industry changed by the new inventions?

   _____

   _____

IMPROVEMENTS IN TRANSPORTATION; THE RAILWAY AGE BEGINS

The invention of the steam engine in 1705 brought in a new source of power. The steam engine used fire to heat water and produce steam. The power of the steam drove the engine. Eventually steam-driven engines were used to run factories and shipping boats.

Starting in the 1820s, steam brought a new burst of industrial growth. George Stephenson, a British engineer, set up the world's first railroad line. It used a steam-driven locomotive. **Henry Bessemer**, a British engineer, devised a way to make steel in large quantities. Railroad rails were made using the inexpensive steel. Soon, railroads were being built all over Britain.

The railroad boom helped business owners move their goods to market more quickly. These changes created thousands of new jobs in several different industries. Millions of British people, including the middle class, also enjoyed the trains. Even Queen Victoria regularly traveled by train.

3. What effects did the invention of the steam engine have?

   _____

   _____

Strategy: Answer the question at the end of each part.

The last page of each lesson of the *Guided Reading Workbook* ends with a graphic organizer that will help you better understand the information in the lesson. Use the graphic organizer to take notes as you read. The notes can help you to prepare for the lesson quiz and Module tests.

Name _____ Class _____ Date _____

Lesson 1, *continued*

As you read this lesson, make notes in the chart to explain how each factor listed contributed to an Industrial Revolution in Great Britain.

1. Agricultural revolution	
2. Abundant natural resources	
3. Political stability	
4. Factors of production	
5. Technological advances in the textile industry	
6. Entrepreneurs	
7. Building of factories	
8. Railroad boom	

© Houghton Mifflin Harcourt Publishing Company

87   Guided Reading Workbook

PROLOGUE: The Rise of Democratic Ideas

The Legacy of Ancient Greece and Rome

Key Terms and People

government system for exercising authority

monarchy government controlled by one person

aristocracy state ruled by the noble class

oligarchy government ruled by a few powerful people

democracy idea that people can govern themselves

direct democracy government in which citizens rule directly and not through representatives

republic government in which citizens elect the leaders who make government decisions

senate aristocratic branch of Rome's government

Before You Read

Recall what you know about democratic ideas.

In this lesson, you will learn how democracy started in Greece and Rome.

As You Read

Use a web diagram to record the contributions of Greece and Rome to democracy.

ATHENS BUILDS A LIMITED DEMOCRACY
How did democracy develop?

Throughout history, people have felt the need for a **government**, or a system for controlling the society. In some societies, people have lived under single rulers, such as kings. This type of rule is called a **monarchy**. These rulers had total power. Other governments that developed included **aristocracy**, which is a state ruled by the noble class. Later as trade expanded, a class of wealthy merchants often ruled a land. This was known as an **oligarchy**. The idea of **democracy**—that people can govern themselves—grew slowly over time.

In the sixth century BCE, a statesman named Solon developed the first democracy in the city-state of Athens. Each year an assembly of citizens elected three nobles to rule Athens. All citizens were able to vote.

Lesson 1, *continued*

Only about one-tenth of the people were citizens. All free adult males were citizens. Women, slaves, and foreign residents could not be citizens.

About a hundred years later, a leader named Cleisthenes increased the power of the assembly. He allowed all citizens to present laws for debate and passage. He also created a council that suggested laws and advised the assembly. Council members were chosen at random.

1. Who were not considered citizens in Athens during the time of Solon?

_____

_____

GREEK DEMOCRACY CHANGES
What changes occurred in Greek democracy?

Athens became the leader of the city-states in the fourth century BCE. Its ruler, Pericles, strengthened democracy. He let citizens, even poor ones, participate in government. This idea is called **direct democracy**.

The Greek city-states had problems and began to fight each other. Then Greece was defeated by armies from the kingdom of Macedonia. This loss ended democracy in Greece.

During this troubled time, several philosophers appeared. Socrates, Plato, and Aristotle developed their ideas on government and society.

2. Why did democracy end in Greece?

_____

_____

ROME DEVELOPS A REPUBLIC
How was the Roman government organized?

Rome began to rise as Greece fell. By 509 BCE, Rome was a **republic**. Citizens

of a republic have the right to vote and to select their leaders. However, voting rights in Rome belonged only to males who were not born slaves or foreigners.

Rome's republican government had separate branches. Two officials called consuls were in charge of the military and the government. The legislative branch was made up of a **senate** and two assemblies. The senate was made up of wealthy landowners. The assemblies had other classes of citizens. In times of trouble, the republic gave complete power to a ruler called a dictator.

3. How was the Roman legislative branch organized?

_____

_____

ROMAN LAW
Why did Romans create a system of laws?

The Romans created a system of laws that they could use throughout their empire.

In 451 BCE, the Romans created the Twelve Tables, the first written collection of Roman laws. The tablets were publicly displayed. Having written laws meant citizens were more protected. The laws were also more fairly administered.

About 1,000 years later, all Roman laws were put together in the Code of Justinian. The Code established the idea of "a government of laws, not of men."

4. Why were the Twelve Tables important?

_____

_____

Name _____ Class _____ Date _____

Lesson 1, *continued*

As you read this lesson, fill in the chart below by naming each person's contribution to the development of democracy in ancient Greece.

Greek Leader	Role in Developing Democracy
1. Solon	
2. Cleisthenes	
3. Pericles	

Use the diagram to give examples and to explain how Roman laws influenced the development of democracy.

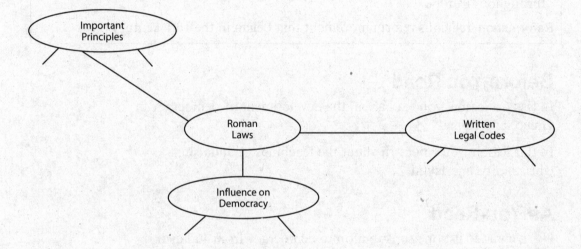

Guided Reading Workbook

PROLOGUE: The Rise of Democratic Ideas

Judeo-Christian Tradition

Key Terms and People

Judaism religion of the Israelites and Jews

Ten Commandments written code of laws

Christianity religion founded by Jesus

Islam religion based on the teachings of Muhammad

Roman Catholic Church church that developed from Christianity

Renaissance cultural movement that started in Italy in the 1300s and spread throughout Europe

Reformation religious reform movement that began in the 16th century

Before You Read

In the last lesson, you read about the development of democracy in Greece and Rome.

In this lesson, you will learn about the teachings of Judaism, Christianity, and Islam.

As You Read

Use a chart to list one contribution to democracy from Judaism, Christianity, Islam, the Renaissance, and the Reformation.

JUDAISM
What is Judaism?

The Israelites were the ancient people who developed **Judaism**. Unlike other groups of people around them, Israelites believed in one God. They also believed that God gave people the freedom to choose between good and evil. So, each person was responsible for his or her own choices. These beliefs led to a new emphasis on the worth of the individual.

The Israelites came to be known as the Jews. They wrote a code of laws that includes the **Ten Commandments**. The Bible says that God gave these laws to Moses on Mount Sinai. These laws focused more on morality and ethics than they did on politics.

The Israelites believed in acting responsibly toward each other. They thought that the community should help the less fortunate. Prophets were leaders and teachers believed by the Jews to be messengers from God. They hoped for a world without poverty or injustice.

1. What are two beliefs of Judaism?

_____

_____

CHRISTIANITY
How did Christianity start?

Jesus was born around 6 to 4 BCE. At this time, the Romans ruled Judea, the homeland of the Jews. Jesus preached the importance of people's love for God, their neighbors, their enemies, and themselves.

In the first century after Jesus' death, his followers started a new religion based on his messages. It was called **Christianity**. The apostle Paul was important in spreading this religion. He preached that all human beings were equal.

The Romans were against both Judaism and Christianity. But these religions spread throughout the Roman Empire. When the Jews rebelled against the Romans, they were forced from their homeland. The Jews then fled to many parts of the world. They carried their beliefs with them.

The emperor Constantine ended the Roman persecution of Christians. He believed God helped him in battle. By 380, Christianity had become the empire's official religion.

2. Why did the Romans stop persecuting Christians?

_____

_____

ISLAM
Who are Muslims?

The religion of **Islam** developed in southwest Asia in the early 600s. The prophet Muhammad taught tolerance and respect.

Followers of Islam are called Muslims. Their holy book is called the Qur'an. In Muslim law, rulers had to follow the same laws as the people they ruled.

Jews and Christians sometimes lived in areas ruled by Muslims. In these places, Muslims had to tolerate their neighbors' religious practices.

3. Why did Muslims tolerate Jews and Christians?

_____

_____

RENAISSANCE AND REFORMATION
How did the Renaissance and Reformation help democracy?

The **Roman Catholic Church** was the church that developed from early Christianity. By the Middle Ages, it was the most powerful institution in Europe. It influenced all parts of life.

In the 1300s, a cultural movement called the **Renaissance** spread through Europe. Artists focused on capturing individual character. Explorers went out to find new lands. Merchants took many risks to gain huge wealth.

The Renaissance also led people to question the Church. This questioning caused the **Reformation**, a protest movement against the power of the Church. It started in Germany as a call for reform. It ended up producing a new division of Christianity—Protestantism.

In Protestant faiths, the clergy did not have special powers. People could find their own way to God. They could read and interpret the Bible for themselves.

The Reformation broke apart the religious unity of Europe. It challenged the authority of Catholic monarchs and popes. It contributed to the growth of democracy.

4. Where did the Reformation begin?

_____

_____

Name _____ Class _____ Date _____

Lesson 2, *continued*

As you read about religious traditions and reactions to them, fill in the chart to identify the democratic ideas that arose from each.

	Influence on the Rise of Democratic Ideas
1. Judaism	
2. Christianity	
3. Islam	
4. Renaissance	
5. Reformation	

PROLOGUE: The Rise of Democratic Ideas

Democracy Develops in England

Key Terms and People

common law body of English law that reflected customs and principles established over time

Magna Carta document drawn up by nobles in 1215 guaranteeing basic political rights in England

due process of law administration of law in known, orderly ways to protect people's rights

Parliament lawmaking body of England

divine right theory that a monarch's power came from God

Glorious Revolution bloodless overthrow of King James II of England and his replacement by William and Mary

constitutional monarchy monarchy in which the ruler's power is limited by law

bill of rights list of rights and freedoms considered essential to the people

Before You Read

In the last lesson, you read about the ideas of Judaism, Christianity, and Islam.

In this lesson, you will learn how democracy developed in England.

As You Read

Use a chart to show the main events in the development of democracy in England.

REFORMS IN MEDIEVAL ENGLAND
How did democracy develop in England?

In 1066, William of Normandy, a French duke, invaded England. He took over the English throne. This change of power eventually ended feudalism and began democracy in England. Feudalism was the political and economic system of the Middle Ages.

An early development in English democracy was a form of trial by jury. It started in the 12th century. These early juries did not decide whether someone was guilty or innocent. Instead, they were asked by a judge to answer questions about the facts of a case.

Common law also helped to develop democracy. The customs and principles of common law were established over time. Common law became the basis of the legal systems in many English-speaking countries, including the United States.

In 1215, King John had trouble with the English nobles. They presented their demands to him in the **Magna Carta**.

This document stated ways the king's power was to be limited. One of the Magna Carta's 63 clauses said that the king could not demand taxes. He had to first ask for approval from the people. Another clause gave an accused person the right to a jury trial. This right has come to be called **due process of law**. Over time, the clause that said the king could not tax people without their consent was understood to mean without the consent of **Parliament**. Parliament made the laws of England.

1. How did the Magna Carta change the way people were taxed?

_____

_____

PARLIAMENT GROWS STRONGER
How did Parliament increase its power?

Over the centuries, Parliament had begun to see itself as a partner to the monarch in governing. Its power had grown. It voted on taxes, passed laws, and advised on royal policies.

In the 17th century, European monarchs claimed that their authority came from God. It was their **divine right**. In England, Parliament clashed with James I. When his son, Charles, became king, Parliament tried to limit royal power with the Petition of Right.

This petition was very important in constitutional history. It demanded an end to taxing without consent, putting citizens in prison illegally, forcing citizens to provide housing for troops, and having a military government in peacetime.

Charles signed the petition. Later, he did not follow the promises he made. This eventually caused civil war in 1642. Several years of fighting followed. The

king's opponents, led by Oliver Cromwell, won control.

2. Why did Parliament force the monarch to sign the Petition of Right?

_____

_____

ESTABLISHMENT OF CONSTITUTIONAL MONARCHY
What was the Glorious Revolution?

Oliver Cromwell ruled briefly. Then, a new Parliament restored the monarchy with Charles II as king. Things had changed, however. The monarch could not tax without Parliament's consent. Also, Parliament passed the *Habeas Corpus* Amendment Act, which kept authorities from wrongly arresting or holding a person.

The next king, James II, believed in the divine right of kings. Within a few years, Parliament withdrew its support of James. It offered the throne to Mary, James's daughter, and her husband, William of Orange. This change in rulers, called the **Glorious Revolution**, showed that Parliament had the right to limit a monarch's power. And it could determine who would take the throne. England became a **constitutional monarchy**. In a constitutional monarchy, a ruler's powers are controlled by a constitution and the laws of the country.

In 1689, William and Mary accepted a **bill of rights** from Parliament. It listed essential rights and freedoms, and it limited the power of the monarchy.

3. What event led to England becoming a constitutional monarchy?

_____

_____

Lesson 3, *continued*

As you read about democratic developments in England, identify how events led to effects that promoted democracy.

Historical Event	Resulting Action or Document	Effect on Democracy
1. King John tried to raise taxes on the nobles.		
2. Edward needed money to pay for war in France.		
3. Seventeenth-century monarchs claimed more power.		
4. Mary and her husband, William of Orange, were offered the throne.		

PROLOGUE: The Rise of Democratic Ideas

The Enlightenment and Democratic Revolutions

Key Terms and People

Enlightenment intellectual movement that started in Europe

social contract agreement between citizens and the government

natural rights rights all people have

separation of powers division of government into separate branches

representative government government in which citizens elect representatives to make laws

federal system government in which powers are divided between federal and state governments

United Nations international organization established in 1945

Before You Read

In the last lesson, you read about the development of democracy in England.

In this lesson, you will learn how new ways of thinking about the rights of people affected democracy in America and France.

As You Read

Use a chart to organize the main ideas and details in the section.

ENLIGHTENMENT THINKERS AND IDEAS
What was the Enlightenment?

The **Enlightenment** was an intellectual movement that developed in Europe in the 17th and 18th centuries. Thinkers of this movement hoped to discover the natural laws that govern society.

One Enlightenment thinker was Thomas Hobbes. He believed that the best form of government was absolute monarchy. He said people should form a type of **social contract**, or agreement, with a ruler. They would submit to a ruler to prevent disorder.

John Locke thought differently. He said all people had **natural rights**, such as the rights to life, liberty, and property. Governments were formed to protect natural rights. Locke said people have a right to rebel against a government that does not protect their rights.

French Enlightenment thinkers included Voltaire, Jean Jacques Rousseau, and Baron de Montesquieu. Voltaire fought for tolerance, freedom of religion, and free speech. Rousseau said the only legitimate government was one in which the people chose what was best for the community.

Lesson 4, *continued*

Montesquieu said that government should be kept under control to protect people's freedoms. He believed that could best be done through a **separation of powers**. This meant dividing the government into branches that would include a lawmaking body, an executive branch to carry out the laws, and courts to interpret laws.

1. According to Locke, why are governments formed?

_____

_____

THE BEGINNINGS OF DEMOCRACY IN AMERICA
How did Enlightenment ideas influence American democracy?

In 1787, a group of American leaders met in Philadelphia. They met to set up a new plan for governing the nation.

Enlightenment ideas helped shape this plan. The U.S. Constitution included a **representative government**, as advocated by Rousseau. This is a government in which citizens elect representatives to make laws for them.

The Constitution created a **federal system**. In this system, the powers of government are divided between the federal and state governments. The Constitution also included a separation of powers between branches in the federal government. This was based on the ideas of Montesquieu.

2. What kind of government did Americans create?

_____

_____

THE FRENCH REVOLUTION
Why did the French revolt?

In the late 1780s, there was great unrest in France. The Enlightenment raised questions about people's rights. The economy was failing, and the peasants were hungry and restless.

In 1789, the common people formed the National Assembly. They felt that they were not represented in their government. Peasants in Paris began an uprising to win democratic freedoms. This fight is known as the French Revolution.

The National Assembly made many reforms. The work of the Assembly did not last long, however. Democracy in France did not develop until the mid-1800s.

3. What was the French Revolution?

_____

_____

THE STRUGGLE FOR DEMOCRACY CONTINUES
How does the United Nations promote democracy?

An international organization called the **United Nations** (UN) was established in 1945. Its goal is to keep world peace and to make people's lives better. In 1948, the UN adopted the Universal Declaration of Human Rights.

This document includes such democratic ideas as the right to life, liberty, and security. It also includes rights to equal protection under the law and the freedom to assemble.

4. What is the Universal Declaration of Human Rights?

_____

_____

Lesson 4, *continued*

As you read about the Enlightenment, take notes to show each thinker's main ideas about government.

Enlightenment Thinker	Ideas About Government
1. Thomas Hobbes	
2. John Locke	
3. Jean Jacques Rousseau	
4. Baron de Montesquieu	

As you read about democratic revolutions, take notes to fill in the Venn diagram below to compare the American Revolution to the French Revolution.

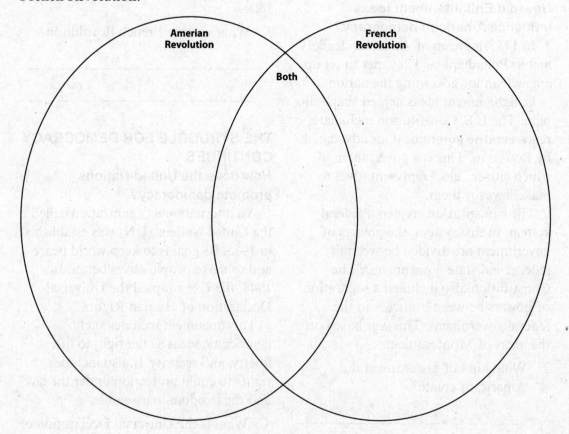

Guided Reading Workbook

Expansion, Exploration, and Encounters

The Mughal Empire in India

Key Terms and People

Babur founder of the Mughal Empire

Mughal name of the empire on the Indian subcontinent founded by Babur

Akbar Mughal emperor with a genius for cultural blending, military conquest, and art; he ruled from 1556 to 1605

Sikh member of a religious group that became the enemy of the Mughals

Shah Jahan Mughal emperor who built Taj Mahal; he ruled from 1628 to 1658

Taj Mahal magnificent tomb built by Shah Jahan for his wife

Aurangzeb last important Mughal emperor, 1658–1707; he expanded the empire but also weakened it

Shivaji Indian warrior king and founder of the Hindu community called Marathas

Before You Read

In the last lesson, you read about how new ways of thinking about the rights of people affected democracy in America and France.

In this lesson, you will read about the establishment of the Mughal Empire in what is now India.

As You Read

Use a chart to identify the Mughal emperors and their successes.

EARLY HISTORY OF THE MUGHALS
How **did the Mughal Empire begin?**

Following the Gupta Empire in the late 400s, India went through a long, unsettled period. Nomads from central Asia invaded the area and created many small kingdoms. In the 700s, Muslims arrived on the scene. This began a long history of fighting with the Hindus who had lived in India for centuries.

After about 300 years, a group of Muslim Turks conquered a region around the city of Delhi. They set up a new empire there. They treated the

Hindus in their area as conquered peoples. Their rule was brought to an end in 1398.

A little over a hundred years later, a new leader named **Babur** raised an army and began to win large parts of India. He was an excellent general. His empire was called the **Mughal** Empire because he and his families were related to the Mongols.

1. Who was Babur?

_____

_____

Lesson 1, *continued*

AKBAR'S GOLDEN AGE
Who was Akbar?

Babur's grandson was **Akbar**. His name means "Great." He ruled with great wisdom and fairness for almost 40 years.

Akbar was a Muslim. However, he believed strongly that people should be allowed to follow the religion they choose. Both Hindus and Muslims worked in the government. He hired people in his government based on their ability.

Akbar ruled fairly. He ended the tax that Hindu pilgrims and all non-Muslims had to pay. To raise money, he taxed people on a percentage of the food they grew. This made it easier for peasants to pay the tax.

He had a strong, well-equipped army that helped him win and keep control of more lands. His empire held about 100 million people—more than lived in all of Europe at the time.

During Akbar's reign, his policy of blending different cultures produced two new languages. One was Hindi, which is widely spoken in India today. The other was Urdu. It is now the official language of Pakistan. The empire became famous for its art, literature, and architecture. He also sponsored the building of a new capital city.

2. What are some examples of Akbar's policy of fair rule?

_____

_____

AKBAR'S SUCCESSORS; THE EMPIRE'S DECLINE AND DECAY
Who ruled after Akbar?

After Akbar's death in 1605, his son Jahangir took control of the Mughal empire. During his reign, the real power was his wife, Nur Jahan. She had a bitter political battle with the **Sikhs**, members of a separate religion based on equality among all people.

The next Mughal ruler was **Shah Jahan**. He too chose not to follow Akbar's policy of religious toleration. Shah Jahan was a great patron of the arts and built many beautiful buildings. One was the famous **Taj Mahal**, a tomb for his wife. His ambitious building plans required high taxes, though. People suffered under his rule.

His son **Aurangzeb** ruled for almost 50 years. He was a devout Muslim, and he punished Hindus and destroyed their temples. This led to a rebellion that took part of his empire. **Shivaji** was an important leader of the Hindu community called Marathas, which set up their own state in southwest India. At the same time, the Sikhs won control of a part of the empire in the northwest.

Aurangzeb used up the empire's resources. People did not feel loyalty to him. As the power of the state weakened, the power of local lords grew. Soon there was only a patchwork of independent states. There continued to be a Mughal emperor, but he was only a figurehead, not a ruler with any real power.

As the Mughal empire was rising and falling, Western traders were building power. Aurangzeb handed them the port of Bombay. This gave India's next conquerors a foothold in India.

3. How did Aurangzeb deal with Hindus?

_____

_____

Name _____ Class_____ Date_____

As you read about the Mughal Empire, make notes in the chart to describe the outcome of each action listed.

1. Babur leads troops to victories over an army led by the sultan of Delhi and the Rajput army.	
2. Akbar governs through a bureaucracy of officials in which natives and foreigners, both Hindus and Muslims, can rise to high office.	
3. Akbar prohibits inheritance of land granted to bureaucrats.	
4. Akbar appoints Rajputs as officers in Mughal army.	
5. Akbar practices cultural blending.	
6. The Sikhs defend Khusrau in his rebellion against his father, Jahangir.	
7. Shah Jahan orders the building of the Taj Mahal.	
8. Aurangzeb strictly enforces Islamic laws and reinstates tax on non-Muslims.	
9. Aurangzeb dies.	

Expansion, Exploration, and Encounters

Europeans Explore the East

Key Terms and People

Prince Henry Portuguese supporter of exploration

Bartolomeu Dias Portuguese explorer who rounded the tip of Africa

Vasco da Gama explorer who gave Portugal a direct sea route to India

Treaty of Tordesillas treaty between Spain and Portugal dividing newly discovered lands between them

Dutch East India Company Dutch company that established and directed trade throughout Asia

Before You Read

In the last lesson, you read about the Mughal Empire in India.

In this lesson, you will read about why and how Europeans began an age of exploration.

As You Read

Use a timeline to take notes on important events in the European exploration of the East.

FOR "GOD, GLORY, AND GOLD"
Why did Europeans begin to explore new lands?

For many centuries, Europeans did not have much contact with people from other lands. That changed in the 1400s. Europeans hoped to gain new sources of wealth. By exploring the seas, traders hoped to find new, faster routes to Asia—the source of spices and luxury goods. Another reason for exploration was spreading Christianity to new lands.

Bernal Diaz del Castillo, an early Spanish explorer, explained his motives: "to serve God and His Majesty, to give light to those who were in darkness and to grow rich as all men desire to do."

Advances in technology made these voyages possible. A new kind of ship, the caravel, was stronger than earlier ships. It had triangle-shaped sails that allowed it to sail against the wind. Ships could now travel far out into the ocean. The magnetic compass allowed sea captains to stay on course better.

1. What were the two main reasons for European exploration?

_____

_____

PORTUGAL LEADS THE WAY; SPAIN ALSO MAKES CLAIMS
How did Portugal lead the way in exploration?

The son of Portugal's king, **Prince Henry**, was committed to the idea of exploring. In 1419, he started a school of navigation. Sea captains, mapmakers, and navigators met and exchanged ideas there. Portugal made the best use of the new sailing technology, and the Portuguese monarchy also invested in overseas exploration.

Over the next few decades, Portuguese captains sailed farther and farther down the west coast of Africa. In 1488, **Bartolomeu Dias** reached the southern tip of Africa. Ten years later, **Vasco da Gama** led a ship around Africa, to India and back. The Portuguese had found a sea route to Asia.

The Spanish, meanwhile, had plans of their own. Christopher Columbus convinced the king and queen that he could reach Asia by sailing west. In 1492, instead of landing in Asia, Columbus touched land in the islands of the Americas. Spain and Portugal argued over which nation had the rights to the land that Columbus had claimed. In 1494, they signed the **Treaty of Tordesillas**. It divided the world into two areas. Portugal won the right to control the eastern parts—including Africa, India, and other parts of Asia. Spain got the western parts—including most of the Americas.

2. How did Spain and Portugal solve their differences over claims to new lands?

_____

_____

_____

TRADING EMPIRES IN THE INDIAN OCEAN
Who established trading empires in the Indian Ocean?

Portugal moved quickly to make the new Indian Ocean route pay off. Through military might, Portugal gained power over islands that were rich in desirable spices. They were called the Spice Islands. Spices now cost Europeans one-fifth of what they had cost before, while still making Portugal very wealthy.

Other European nations joined in this trade. In the 1600s, the English and Dutch entered the East Indies. They quickly broke Portuguese power in the area. Then both nations set up an East India Company to control Asian trade. These companies were more than businesses. They were like governments. They had the power to make money, sign treaties, and raise their own armies. The **Dutch East India Company** was richer and more powerful than England's company.

By 1700, the Dutch ruled much of Indonesia. They had trading posts in many other Asian countries and commanded the southern tip of Africa. At the same time, both England and France finally gained footholds in India.

Nevertheless, even though Europeans controlled the trade between Asia and Europe, they had little impact on most people living in these areas.

3. How did the Dutch and English become Indian Ocean trading powers?

_____

_____

_____

As you read about the age of exploration, take notes to answer
questions about events listed in the timeline.

1400			1. What technological advances made possible the age of exploration?
1419	**Prince Henry starts a navigation school.**		
1487	**Bartolomeu Dias rounds the southern tip of Africa.**		2. What were some immediate and some long-term outcomes of Columbus's voyage?
1492	**Columbus reaches the Caribbean.**		
1494	**Spain and Portugal sign the Treaty of Tordesillas.**		3. What was the most important result of this agreement?
1498	**Vasco da Gama reaches the port of Calicut on the Indian Ocean.**		
1500			4. How did Portugal benefit from his voyage?
1521	**Ferdinand Magellan leads a Spanish expedition to the Philippines.**		
1565	**Spain begins settlements in the Philippines.**		5. Why did Spain set up trading posts in Asia?
1600			6. How did the Dutch gain control of much of the Indian Ocean trade?
1619	**The Dutch establish a trading center on Java.**		
1664	**France sets up its own East India Company.**		7. How did the European battles for Indian Ocean trade affect the peoples of Asia before the 19th century?

Expansion, Exploration, and Encounters

China and Japan Reject Expansion

Key Terms and People

Hongwu commander of the rebel army that drove the Mongols out of China in 1368

Ming Dynasty Chinese dynasty that ruled from 1368 to 1644

Yonglo Ming ruler; son of Hongwu

Zheng He Muslim admiral who led seven exploration voyages during the Ming Dynasty

Manchus people from Manchuria

Qing Dynasty Chinese dynasty begun by the Manchus that followed the Ming Dynasty

Kangxi powerful Manchu emperor of the Qing Dynasty

daimyo Japanese warrior-chieftain who commanded a private army of samurai

Oda Nobunaga daimyo who hoped to control all of Japan and seized Kyoto

Toyotomi Hideyoshi daimyo who took control of almost all of Japan

kabuki type of Japanese theater

haiku type of Japanese poetry

Tokugawa Shogunate dynasty that ruled Japan from 1603 to 1868

Before You Read

In the last lesson, you read about European exploration in the East.

In this lesson, you will read about China and Japan's political and social development and efforts to limit contact with Europe.

As You Read

Use a chart to take notes about China and Japan's contact with Europe.

CHINA UNDER THE POWERFUL MING DYNASTY; MANCHUS FOUND THE QING DYNASTY; LIFE IN MING AND QING CHINA
What was life like in China under the Ming and Qing?

Mongol rule in China ended in 1368 when **Hongwu** took control of the country. He declared himself the first emperor of the **Ming Dynasty**. Hongwu began his rule by increasing the amount of food produced and improving the government. His son **Yonglo** continued his better policies. Under Yonglo, an admiral named **Zheng He** led several voyages to Southeast Asia, India,

Arabia, and Africa. Wherever he went, he gave away gifts to show Chinese superiority.

The Ming government eventually tried to isolate China from the world, but Europeans continued to trade for Chinese ceramics and silk. Missionaries brought Christianity and technology.

By 1600, the Ming Dynasty had weakened and the **Manchus**, from Manchuria, northeast of China, took control in 1644. They started the **Qing Dynasty**. Two important emperors were **Kangxi** and his grandson Qian-long. They brought China to its largest size, increased its wealth, and sponsored an increase in artistic production.

During the Ming and Qing dynasties, farming methods, food production and nutrition improved. This caused the population to grow.

In Chinese culture, females were not valued. Many infant girls were killed, and adult women had few rights.

The Chinese tried to preserve their traditions and their isolation. Artists created works that showed traditional Chinese values and ideas. This helped to unify the Chinese people.

1. Which parts of society improved during this time, and which continued to be the same?

_____

_____

A NEW FEUDALISM UNDER STRONG LEADERS; LIFE IN TOKUGAWA JAPAN; CONTACT BETWEEN EUROPE AND JAPAN; THE CLOSED COUNTRY POLICY
Why were warriors fighting in Japan?

From 1467 to 1568, Japan entered a long, dark period of civil war. Powerful warriors took control of large areas of

land. They were called **daimyo**. They fought each other constantly to gain land and more power.

In 1568, one of the daimyo, **Oda Nobunaga**, took control of Kyoto. It was the site of the emperor's capital. His general, **Toyotomi Hideyoshi**, continued to try to bring all of Japan under one rule. Using military conquest and clever diplomacy, he won that goal in 1590.

Tokugawa Ieyasu completed the unification of Japan. He became the shogun, or sole ruler. He moved the capital to what would become Tokyo.

The new government brought about a long period of peace and prosperity for most people. Many peasant farmers, however, did not prosper, and left the countryside to move to the cities.

A traditional culture thrived, but in cities, new styles emerged. Townspeople attended **kabuki**, dramas of urban life. They also read **haiku**, poetry that presents images instead of ideas.

In the mid-1500s, European traders and missionaries began to arrive in Japan. Some missionaries, however, scorned traditional Japanese beliefs. They also got involved in local politics. In 1612, Tokugawa banned Christianity from the country. Christians were persecuted. This was part of a larger plan to protect the country from European influence. For the next 200 years, Japan remained closed to most European contact. All of Japan's shoguns who ruled during this time descended from Tokugawa Ieyasu and were part of the **Tokugawa Shogunate**.

2. Which three leaders helped bring Japan under one rule?

_____

_____

Name _____ Class_____ Date_____

As you read this lesson, take notes to answer questions about the Ming Dynasty in China and life under Tokugawa rule in Japan.

The rulers of the Ming Dynasty drive out the Mongols and bring peace and prosperity to China.

1. How did Hongwu bring stability to China? →	2. What were some of his agricultural reforms?
3. Why was only the government allowed to conduct foreign trade? →	4. How did foreign trade affect Ming China?

How did each of the following influence Japanese society and culture?

5. Tokugawa Shogunate →	6. Portuguese
7. Christian missionaries →	8. "Closed country" policy

Expansion, Exploration, and Encounters

Spain Builds an American Empire

Key Terms and People

Christopher Columbus Italian explorer, sailing for Spain, who landed in the Americas

colony land controlled by another nation

Hernando Cortés conquistador who defeated the Aztec Empire, conquering Mexico

conquistadors Spanish explorers who conquered the Americas in the 16th century

Francisco Pizarro conquistador who defeated the Incan Empire, conquering Peru

Atahualpa last Incan emperor, defeated and killed by the Spanish

mestizo person with mixed Spanish and Native American blood

encomienda system of mining and farming using natives as slave labor

Before You Read

In the last lesson, you read about China and Japan's development.

In this lesson, you will read about the Spanish and Portuguese exploration of the Americas.

As You Read

Use a timeline to trace the major events in the establishment of Spain's empire in the Americas.

THE VOYAGES OF COLUMBUS
How did the voyage of Columbus change the Americas?

In 1492, **Christopher Columbus**, an Italian sailor, led a voyage for Spain. He sailed west hoping to reach Asia. Instead, he landed in the Americas. Columbus thought that he had reached the East Indies in Asia. He misnamed the natives he met there, calling them Indians. He claimed the land for Spain. From then on, Spain began to create **colonies**. Colonies are lands controlled by another nation.

In 1500, a Portuguese explorer claimed Brazil. In 1501, Amerigo Vespucci explored the eastern coast of South America. He said that these lands were a new world. Soon after, a mapmaker showed the lands as a separate continent. He named them America after Vespucci.

Other voyages gave Europeans more knowledge about the world. Spanish explorer Vasco Núñez de Balboa reached the Pacific Ocean. Portuguese explorer Ferdinand Magellan sailed completely around the world.

1. Which voyages gave Europeans new knowledge of the world?

_____

_____

2. Give two examples of conquistadors and explain what they did.

_____

_____

SPANISH CONQUESTS IN MEXICO; SPANISH CONQUESTS IN PERU
How did Spain build an empire?

Hernando Cortés was one of the Spanish **conquistadors**, or conquerors. In the 16th century, they began to explore the lands of the Americas. They were seeking great riches. In 1519, Cortés came to Mexico and defeated the powerful Aztec Empire led by Montezuma II.

About 15 years later, **Francisco Pizarro** led another Spanish force. It conquered the mighty Inca Empire of South America, led by **Atahualpa**, the last of the Incan emperors. Once again, the Spanish found gold and silver. By the mid-1500s, Spain had formed an American empire that stretched from modern-day Mexico to Peru.

The Spanish lived among the people they conquered. Spanish men married native women. Their children and descendants were called **mestizo**—people with mixed Spanish and Native American blood. The Spanish also formed large farms and mines that used natives as slave labor. This system was known as *encomienda*.

One large area of the Americas—Brazil—was the possession of Portugal. In the 1530s, colonists began to settle there. Colonists built huge farms called plantations to grow sugar, which was in demand in Europe.

SPAIN'S INFLUENCE EXPANDS
Where did Spain hope to gain more power?

Soon Spain began to want even more power in the Americas. It started to look at land that is now part of the United States. Explorers like Coronado led expeditions to the area. Catholic priests went along and converted some of the Native Americans.

3. What area did Coronado explore?

_____

_____

OPPOSITION TO SPANISH RULE
Who opposed Spanish rule?

As Spanish priests worked to convert the natives, they began to make some protests about their treatment. One thing they criticized was the *encomienda* system. A monk named Bartolomé de Las Casas and others successfully called for the end of the system.

Native Americans also resisted new or continued Spanish rule. One of the most serious rebellions occurred in New Mexico. A Pueblo leader named Popé led the effort. It involved about 17,000 warriors and drove the Spanish back into New Spain for 12 years.

4. What challenges to their power did the Spanish face?

_____

_____

Guided Reading Workbook

Lesson 4, *continued*

As you read about the empire Spain built in the Americas, take notes to answer questions about the timeline below.

1492	**Christopher Columbus sails westward from Spain, hoping to reach Asia.**	1. What was the significance of Columbus's voyages?
1519	**Ferdinand Magellan sets sail on a voyage that rounds the southern tip of South America.**	2. Magellan himself died in the Philippines. What was the importance of the voyage his crew completed?
1521	**Hernando Cortés conquers the Aztec.**	3. What factors helped the Spanish defeat the Aztec?
		4. How did the Spanish treat the peoples they conquered?
1533	**Francisco Pizarro conquers the Inca Empire.**	5. What was unique about the Spanish colonization of the lands of New Mexico?
1540	**Francisco Vásquez de Coronado explores the Southwest.**	6. What was the long-term consequence of this action?
1542	**Spain abolishes the *encomienda* system.**	

Expansion, Exploration, and Encounters

European Nations Settle North America

Key Terms and People

New France area of the Americas explored and claimed by France

Jamestown first permanent English settlement in North America

Pilgrims group of English people who founded the colony of Plymouth in 1620

Puritans group of English people who founded a colony at Massachusetts Bay in 1630

New Netherland Dutch colony begun in an area that is now New York

French and Indian War war between Britain and France over land in North America

Metacom Native American leader who led an attack on the villages of Massachusetts; also called King Philip

Before You Read

In the last lesson, you read about Spanish conquests in the Americas.

In this lesson, you will read about how other nations competed for power in North America.

As You Read

Use a chart to record information about early settlements in North America.

COMPETING CLAIMS IN NORTH AMERICA

***What* new colonies were formed in North America?**

In the early 1500s, the French began to explore North America. Jacques Cartier discovered and named the St. Lawrence River. He then followed it to the site of what is now Montreal. In 1608, Samuel de Champlain sailed as far as modern-day Quebec. In the next 100 years, the French explored and claimed the area around the Great Lakes and the Mississippi River all the way to its mouth at the Gulf of Mexico. The area became known as **New France**. The main activity in this colony was trading in fur.

1. What was the main economic activity in New France?

_____

_____

THE ENGLISH ARRIVE IN NORTH AMERICA

Why did the English settle in Massachusetts?

The English also began to colonize North America. The first permanent settlement was at **Jamestown**, in modern Virginia, in 1607. The colony struggled at first. Many settlers died from disease, hunger, or war with the native peoples. Soon, farmers began to grow tobacco to meet the high demand for it in Europe.

In 1620, a group known as **Pilgrims** founded a second English colony in Plymouth, in Massachusetts. These settlers and others who followed were deeply religious people who did not agree with the practices of the Church of England. They were called **Puritans**.

Meanwhile, the Dutch also started a new colony. They settled in the location of modern New York and called it **New Netherland**. Like the French, they traded fur. The colony became known as a home to people of many different cultures. Europeans also took possession of many islands of the Caribbean. There they built tobacco and sugar plantations that used enslaved Africans as workers.

2. In which two places did English colonists first settle?

_____

_____

THE STRUGGLE FOR NORTH AMERICA; NATIVE AMERICANS RESPOND

How did native peoples respond to the colonists?

The European powers began to fight for control of North America. First, the English forced the Dutch to give up their colony. New Netherland was renamed New York. The English also started other colonies along the Atlantic coast, and pushed westward. There the English colonists interfered with North American French settlers.

The British and the French clashed over the Ohio Valley in 1754. The fight was called the **French and Indian War**. When it ended in 1763, France was forced to give up all its land in North America to England.

The native peoples responded to the colonists in many different ways. Many worked closely with the French and Dutch, joining in the fur trade and benefiting from it. Native Americans had stormier relations with English colonists. More than just trade, the English wanted to settle the land and farm it. This was land that Native Americans would not be able to use for hunting or growing their own food.

Conflicts over land erupted into war several times. One of the bloodiest conflicts was known as King Philip's War. The Native American ruler **Metacom** (also known as King Philip) led an attack on colonial villages throughout Massachusetts. After a year of fierce fighting, the British colonists defeated the Native Americans.

As in Spanish lands, the native peoples suffered even more from disease than from warfare. Thousands of Native Americans died from European illnesses. This made it impossible for them to resist the growth of the colonies.

3. Why did Native Americans lose their way of life?

_____

_____

Name _____ Class_____ Date_____

As you read this lesson, fill out the chart below by writing notes that describe aspects of each European settlement.

1. New France	
Explorers	Reasons for exploration

2. Jamestown	
Founders	Significance of colony

3. Plymouth and Massachusetts Bay colonies	
Settlers	Reasons for colonization

4. New Netherland	
Land claims	Reasons for colonization

Expansion, Exploration, and Encounters

The Atlantic Slave Trade

Key Terms and People

Atlantic slave trade buying and selling of Africans for work in the Americas

indentured servitude a system of labor by which a person could work to pay off the cost of coming to the Americas

triangular trade European trade between the Americas, Africa, and Europe involving slaves and other goods

Middle Passage voyage that brought captured Africans to the West Indies and the Americas

Before You Read

In the last lesson, you read about how different European nations settled in North America.

In this lesson, you will read about the slave trade that brought Africans to the Americas.

As You Read

Use an outline to list causes and effects of the Atlantic slave trade.

THE CAUSES OF AFRICAN SLAVERY

What was the Atlantic slave trade?

Slavery has had a long history in Africa and in the world. In the seventh century, Muslim rulers in North Africa enslaved non-Muslim Africans. Muslim traders also started to take many slaves to Southwest Asia.

Most worked as servants, and they did have certain rights. Also, the sons and daughters of slaves were considered to be free. The European slave trade that began in the 1500s was larger. The enslaved Africans also were treated far more harshly.

In the Americas, Europeans first used Native Americans to work farms and mines. When the native peoples began dying from disease, the Europeans brought in Africans. The buying and selling of Africans for work in the Americas became known as the **Atlantic slave trade**. From 1500 to 1870, when the slave trade in the Americas finally ended, about 9.5 million Africans had been imported as slaves. The African slave trade differed from another colonial system of labor called **indentured servitude**. Indentured servants came to the Americas voluntarily and worked for an employer for a certain period. African slaves were brought to the Americas against their will and were slaves for life.

The Spanish first began the practice of bringing Africans to the Americas. However, the Portuguese increased the

Lesson 6, *continued*

demand for slaves. They were looking for workers for their sugar plantations in Brazil.

1. Why were slaves brought to the Americas?

_____

_____

SLAVERY SPREADS THROUGHOUT THE AMERICAS; A FORCED JOURNEY
What kinds of trade included human beings?

Other European colonies also brought slaves to work on tobacco, sugar, and coffee plantations. About 400,000 slaves were brought to the English colonies in North America. Their population had increased to about 2 million in 1830.

Many African rulers joined in the slave trade. They captured people inland and brought them to the coast to sell to European traders.

Africans taken to the Americas were part of a **triangular trade** between Europe, Africa, and the Americas. European ships brought manufactured goods to Africa, trading them for captured Africans. They carried the Africans across the Atlantic to the Americas, where they were sold into slavery. The traders then bought sugar, coffee, and tobacco to bring back to Europe.

Another triangle involved ships sailing from the northern English colonies in North America. They carried rum to Africa, Africans to the West Indies, and sugar and molasses back to the colonies to make more rum.

The part of the voyage that brought captured Africans to the Americas was called the **Middle Passage**. It was harsh and cruel. Africans were crammed into

ships, beaten, and given little food. About 20 percent of the people on these ships died.

2. What was the triangular trade?

_____

_____

SLAVERY IN THE AMERICAS; CONSEQUENCES OF THE SLAVE TRADE
What was life like for the slaves?

Life on the plantations was harsh as well. People were sold to the highest bidder. They worked from dawn to dusk in the fields. They lived in small huts and had little food and clothing. Africans kept alive their traditional music and beliefs to try to maintain their spirits. Sometimes they rebelled. From North America to Brazil, from 1522 to the 1800s, there were small-scale slave revolts.

The Atlantic slave trade had a huge impact on both Africa and the Americas. In Africa many cultures lost generations of members. Africans began fighting Africans over the control of the slave trade.

The Africans' labor helped build the Americas. They brought skills and culture, too. Many of the nations of the Americas have mixed-race populations.

3. How did Africans change the Americas?

_____

_____

Name _____ Class _____ Date _____

Lesson 6, *continued*

As you read this lesson, write notes to answer questions about the causes and consequences of the enslavement of Africans.

How did each of the following contribute to the development of the Atlantic slave trade?	
1. European colonization of the Americas	2. Portuguese settlement of Brazil
3. African rulers	4. African merchants

What were the consequences of the Atlantic slave trade for each of the following?	
5. African societies	6. Enslaved Africans
7. American colonies	8. Present-day American cultures

Guided Reading Workbook

Expansion, Exploration, and Encounters

The Columbian Exchange and Global Trade

Key Terms and People

Columbian Exchange global transfer of foods, plants, and animals during the colonization of the Americas

capitalism economic system based on private ownership and the investment of wealth for profit

joint-stock company company in which people pooled their wealth for a common purpose

mercantilism economic policy of increasing wealth and power by obtaining large amounts of gold and silver and selling more goods than are bought

favorable balance of trade condition resulting from selling more goods than are bought

Before You Read

In the last lesson, you read about the Atlantic slave trade.

In this lesson, you will read about other kinds of trade.

As You Read

Use a chart to take notes on how the Columbian Exchange and global trade changed Europe.

THE COLUMBIAN EXCHANGE
What was the Columbian Exchange?

There was constant movement of people and products from Europe and Africa to the Americas. The large-scale transfer of foods, plants, and animals was called the **Columbian Exchange**. Important foods such as corn and potatoes were taken from the Americas to Europe, Africa, and Asia.

Some foods moved from the Old World to the New. Bananas, black-eyed peas, and yams were taken from Africa to the Americas. Cattle, pigs, and horses had never been seen in the Americas

until the Europeans brought them. Deadly illnesses also moved to the Americas. They killed a large part of the Native American population.

1. What did the Columbian Exchange take from the Americas, and what did it bring?

_____

_____

Lesson 7, *continued*

GLOBAL TRADE
How did business change?

The settling of the Americas and the growth of trade started an economic revolution. This revolution led to new business practices still followed today. One was the rise of an economic system called **capitalism**. It is based on private ownership and the right of a business to earn a profit on money invested.

Another new business idea was the **joint-stock company**. In this type of company, many investors pool their money to start a business and share in the profits.

2. What is capitalism?

_____

_____

THE GROWTH OF MERCANTILISM
Why were colonies important in mercantilism?

During the Commercial Revolution, European governments began to follow an idea called **mercantilism**. According to this theory, a country's power depended on its wealth. Getting more gold and silver increased a country's wealth; so did selling more goods than it bought. Selling more than it buys results in a **favorable balance of trade** for a country. Colonies played an important role because they provided goods that could be sold in trade.

The American colonies changed European society. Merchants grew wealthy and powerful. Towns and cities grew larger. Still, most people lived in the countryside, farmed for a living, and were poor.

3. Why were colonies important to European mercantilism?

_____

_____

Guided Reading Workbook

Name _____ Class _____ Date _____

As you read, note some cause-and-effect relationships relating to the European colonization of the Americas.

Causes	Event/Trend	Effects
	1. Columbian Exchange	
	2. Global trade	
	3. Inflation	
	4. Formation of joint-stock companies	
	5. Growth of mercantilism	

Absolute Monarchs in Europe

Spain's Empire and European Absolutism

Key Terms and People

Philip II Spanish king who took control of Portugal but failed in his invasion of England

absolute monarch king or queen with complete control

divine right idea that a ruler receives the right to rule from God

Before You Read

In the last lesson, you read about global trade resulting from the colonization of the Americas.

In this lesson, you will learn about changes occurring in Europe in the 1500s and 1600s.

As You Read

Use a chart to record causes and effects of events in Europe.

A POWERFUL SPANISH EMPIRE
How did Spain's power increase and then decrease?

Charles V of Spain ruled the Holy Roman Empire and other European countries. In 1556, he left the throne and split his holdings. His brother Ferdinand received Austria and the Holy Roman Empire. His son, **Philip II**, got Spain and its colonies.

Philip II then took control of Portugal when the king of Portugal, his uncle, died without an heir. Philip also got its global territories in Africa, India, and the East Indies. When he tried to invade England in 1588, though, he failed. The defeat made Spain weaker. However, Spain still seemed strong because of the wealth—gold and silver—that flowed in from its colonies in the Americas.

1. Who was Philip II?

_____

_____

GOLDEN AGE OF SPANISH ART AND LITERATURE
How did works from the golden age of Spanish art and literature reflect the values and attitudes of the period?

Spain's great wealth allowed monarchs and nobles to become patrons of artists. Two of the greatest artists of the 16th and 17th century were El Greco and Diego Velásquez. El Greco's work reflected the religious faith of Spain during this period. The paintings of Velásquez reflected the pride of the Spanish monarchy.

Lesson 1, *continued*

In literature, Miguel de Cervantes wrote *Don Quixote de la Mancha,* which ushered in the birth of the modern European novel. The novel tells the story of a Spanish nobleman who reads too many books about heroic knights.

2. Who were some of the artists and writers of Spain's golden age?

_____

_____

THE SPANISH EMPIRE WEAKENS
What weakened the Spanish Empire?

Spain's new wealth led to some serious problems. The prices of goods constantly rose. Unfair taxes kept the poor from building up any wealth of their own. As prices rose, Spaniards bought more goods from other lands. To finance their wars, Spanish kings had to borrow money from banks in foreign countries. The silver from the colonies began to flow to Spain's enemies.

In the middle of these troubles, Spain lost land. Seven provinces of the Spanish Netherlands rose in protest against high taxes and attempts to crush Protestantism in the Netherlands. These seven provinces were Protestant, whereas Spain was strongly Catholic. In 1579, they declared their independence from Spain and became the United Provinces of the Netherlands. The ten southern provinces (present-day Belgium) were Catholic and remained under Spanish control.

3. Why did Spain lose power?

_____

_____

THE INDEPENDENT DUTCH PROSPER
Why did the Dutch prosper?

The United Provinces of the Netherlands was different from other European states of the time. It was a republic, not a kingdom. Each province had a leader elected by the people.

The Dutch also practiced religious tolerance, letting people worship as they wished. Dutch merchants established a trading empire. They had the largest fleet of merchant ships in the world. They were also the most important bankers in Europe.

4. Give two reasons for the success of the Dutch in trading.

_____

_____

ABSOLUTISM IN EUROPE
What is absolutism?

Though he lost his Dutch possessions, Philip II continued to hold tight control over Spain. He wanted to control the lives of his people. Philip and others who ruled in the same way were called **absolute monarchs**. They believed in holding all power. They also believed in **divine right**. This is the idea that a ruler receives the right to rule from God.

Widespread unrest in Europe in the 17th century led to an increase in absolute rule, or absolutism, and its restrictions. Absolute rulers used their increased power to impose order. They wanted to free themselves from the limitations imposed by the nobility and government bodies.

5. What did absolute monarchs believe?

_____

_____

Name _____ Class _____ Date _____

As you read about the Spanish empire, briefly note the causes or effects (depending on which is missing) of each event or situation.

Causes	Effects
1. The gold and silver coming from its vast empire made Spain incredibly wealthy.	
2.	Spain suffered from severe inflation.
3.	The Spanish economy declined and at times Spain was bankrupt.
4. Philip raised taxes in the Netherlands and tried to crush Protestantism.	
5.	The Dutch became wealthy from trade and banking.
6.	European monarchs became increasingly powerful.

Absolute Monarchs in Europe

The Reign of Louis XIV

Key Terms and People

Edict of Nantes order that gave Huguenots the right to live in peace in Catholic France

Cardinal Richelieu chief minister of France who reduced the power of the nobles

skepticism belief that nothing could be known for certain

Louis XIV French king who was an absolute ruler

intendant official of the French government

Jean Baptiste Colbert chief minister of finance under Louis XIV

War of the Spanish Succession war fought by other European nations against France and Spain when those two states tried to unite their thrones

Before You Read

In the last lesson, you were introduced to the idea of absolutism.

In this lesson, you will read about absolute power in France.

As You Read

Use a chart to list major events involving the French monarchy.

RELIGIOUS WARS AND POWER STRUGGLES; WRITERS TURN TOWARD SKEPTICISM
What changes were occurring in France?

France was torn by eight religious wars between Catholics and Protestants from 1562 to 1598.

In 1589, a Protestant prince, Henry of Navarre, became King Henry IV. He changed religions, becoming a Catholic to please the majority of his people. In 1598, he issued an order called the **Edict of Nantes**. It gave Huguenots—French Protestants—the right to live in peace and have their own churches in some cities.

Henry rebuilt the French economy and brought peace to the land. He was followed by his son, Louis XIII, a weak king. However, Louis had a very capable chief minister, **Cardinal Richelieu**. Richelieu ruled the land for Louis and increased the power of the crown.

The cardinal ordered the Huguenots not to build walls around their cities. He also said nobles had to destroy their castles. As a result, Protestants and nobles could not hide within walls to defy the king's power. Richelieu gave extra power to government workers who came from the middle class—reducing the power of the nobles.

French thinkers had reacted to the religious wars with horror. They developed a new philosophy called **skepticism**. Nothing could be known for certain, they argued. Doubting old ideas was the first step to learning the truth, they said. Two important French skeptics were Michel de Montaigne and René Descartes. These writers argued that all beliefs should be questioned.

1. How did the monarchy get stronger in France?

_____

_____

LOUIS XIV COMES TO POWER
How did Louis XIV rule?

In 1643, **Louis XIV** became king at the age of four. Cardinal Mazarin, who succeeded Richelieu as minister, ruled for Louis until he was 22. Louis became a powerful ruler who had total control of France. He was determined to never let nobles challenge him.

He kept the nobles out of his councils. He gave more power to government officials called **intendants** and made sure that they answered only to him. He also worked hard to increase the wealth of France. His minister of finance, **Jean Baptiste Colbert**, tried to build French industry. Colbert wanted to persuade French people to buy French-made goods and not those from other countries. He urged people to settle in the new French colony of Canada in North America. The fur trade there brought wealth to France.

2. How did Louis XIV make sure he kept his power?

_____

_____

THE SUN KING'S GRAND STYLE; LOUIS FIGHTS DISASTROUS WARS
What changes did Louis make?

Louis XIV enjoyed a life of luxury at his court. He built a huge and beautiful palace at Versailles near Paris. He promoted art that glorified himself and strengthened his absolute rule. He made opera and ballet more popular and supported writers like Molière. Nobles had to depend on Louis's favor to advance in society.

Louis made France the most powerful nation in Europe. France had a larger population and a bigger army than any other country. However, Louis made some mistakes that later proved costly. After winning some wars against neighboring countries, he became bolder and tried to seize more land. Other nations allied to form a group called the League of Augsburg to stop France in the late 1680s. The high cost of these wars, combined with poor harvests, produced problems at home in France.

The final war fought in Louis's time was fought over succession to the throne of Spain and lasted from 1700 to 1713. In this **War of the Spanish Succession**, France and Spain attempted to set up united thrones. The rest of Europe felt threatened and joined in war against them. Both France and Spain were forced to give up some of their American and European colonies to England. England became the new rising power. France's staggering debt, high taxes, and abuses of power would eventually lead to revolution.

3. How did Louis XIV bring disaster to France?

_____

_____

Lesson 2, *continued*

As you read about the French monarchy, write notes to answer the questions.

Wars between the Huguenots and Catholics create chaos in France.	
1. How did Henry of Navarre end the crisis and restore order?	
2. How did Cardinal Richelieu strengthen the French monarchy?	
3. What effect did the religious wars have on French intellectuals?	

Louis XIV became the most powerful monarch of his time.	
4. What steps did Jean Baptiste Colbert take to turn France into an economic power?	
5. In what ways did Louis XIV support the arts?	
6. Why did Louis fail in his attempts to expand the French empire?	
7. What was the legacy of Louis XIV?	

Central European Monarchs Clash

Key Terms and People

Thirty Years' War conflict over religion, territory, and power among European ruling families

Maria Theresa empress of Austria whose main enemy was Prussia

Frederick the Great leader of Prussia who sought to increase his territory

Seven Years' War conflict from 1756 to 1763 in which the forces of Britain and Prussia battled those of Austria, France, Russia, and other countries

Before You Read

In the last lesson, you read about how absolute power grew in France.

In this lesson, you will learn about absolutism in Austria and Prussia.

As You Read

Use a chart to list the effects of events occurring in central Europe.

THE THIRTY YEARS' WAR
***What* caused the Thirty Years' War?**

In the late 16th and early 17th centuries, both Lutheran and Catholic princes in Germany tried to gain followers. In 1608, Lutherans joined together to form the Protestant Union. The next year, Catholic princes formed the Catholic League. Relations between sides became tense. Then in 1618, a war broke out and lasted for 30 terrible years. It was called the **Thirty Years' War**.

During the first half of the war, Catholic forces led by Ferdinand, the Holy Roman Emperor, won. However, Germany suffered because he allowed his large army to loot towns. Then the Protestant king of Sweden, Gustavus Adolphus, won several battles against him.

In the last years of the long war, France helped the Protestants. Although France was a Catholic nation, Richelieu feared the growing power of the Hapsburg family.

The Thirty Years' War ended in 1648 with the Peace of Westphalia. It had been a disaster for Germany. About 4 million people had died, and the economy was in ruins. It took Germany two centuries to recover.

The peace treaty weakened the power of Austria and Spain. But it made France stronger. The French gained German territory. The treaty also made German princes independent of the Holy Roman Emperor. It ended religious wars in Europe. Lastly, the treaty introduced a new way of negotiating peace—a method still used today. All states involved in the fighting meet to settle the problems of a war and decide the terms of peace.

The most important result of the Thirty Years' War was the transformation of Europe into a group of *nation-states*. Nation-states are equal, independent states, each with the power to set up an army and govern its people.

1. What were three results of the Thirty Years' War?

   _____

   _____

STATES FORM IN CENTRAL EUROPE
Who ruled Austria?

The formation of strong states took place slowly in central Europe. The economies there were less developed than in western Europe. Most people were still peasants. This region had not built an economy based on cities and commercialism. Nobles enjoyed great influence. This helped them keep the serfs on the land and prevent the rise of strong rulers. Still, two important states arose.

The Hapsburg family ruled Austria, Hungary, and Bohemia. Their empire linked many different peoples—Czechs, Hungarians, Italians, Croatians, and Germans. To make sure Hapsburg control continued, Charles VI, the Hapsburg ruler, made his daughter **Maria Theresa** heir to the empire. She was opposed by the kings of Prussia, a new powerful state in northern Germany.

2. Who were the Hapsburgs?

   _____

   _____

PRUSSIA CHALLENGES AUSTRIA
What was Prussia?

Like Austria, Prussia rose to power in the late 1600s. Like the Hapsburgs of Austria, Prussia's ruling family, the Hohenzollerns, also had ambitions.

Prussia was a strong state that gave much power to its large, well-trained army. In 1740, **Frederick the Great** of Prussia invaded one of Maria Theresa's lands. Austria fought hard to keep the territory but lost. Still, in fighting the War of the Austrian Succession, Maria Theresa managed to keep the rest of her empire intact.

The two sides fought again, beginning in 1756. In the **Seven Years' War**, Austria abandoned Britain, its old ally, for France and Russia. Prussia joined with Britain. The Prussians and British won. In that victory, Britain gained economic domination of India.

3. What effect did fighting between Austria and Prussia have on Britain?

   _____

   _____

Name _____ Class_____ Date_____

As you read about the absolute monarchs who ruled in central Europe, fill out the chart by writing notes in the appropriate spaces.

The Thirty Years' War	
1. Note two causes of the war.	
2. Note four consequences of the war and the Peace of Westphalia.	

Central Europe	
3. Note two differences between the economies of western and central Europe.	
4. Note two reasons why central European empires were weak.	

Prussia and Austria	
5. Note three steps the Hapsburgs took to become more powerful.	
6. Note three steps the Hohenzollerns took to build up their state.	

Guided Reading Workbook

Absolute Monarchs in Europe

Lesson 4

Absolute Rulers of Russia

Key Terms and People

Ivan the Terrible ruler who added lands to Russia, gave it a code of laws, and also used his secret police to execute "traitors"

boyar Russian noble who owned land

Peter the Great important leader of Russia who started westernization

westernization use of western Europe as a model of change

Before You Read

In the last lesson, you read about how Austria and Prussia became strong states.

In this lesson, you will learn how Russia developed into a powerful state.

As You Read

Use a chart to list ways Peter the Great solved problems facing Russia.

THE FIRST CZAR
Who was Ivan the Terrible?

Ivan III had begun centralizing the Russian government. His son, Vasily, continued the work of adding territory to the growing Russian state. Ivan's grandson, Ivan IV, was called **Ivan the Terrible**. He came to the throne in 1533, when he was three years old.

At first, landowning nobles, known as **boyars**, tried to control Ivan. Eventually, he ruled successfully on his own. He added lands to Russia and gave the country a code of laws. After his wife, Anastasia, died, however, his rule turned harsh. He used secret police to hunt down enemies and kill them. Ivan even murdered his oldest son.

A few years after he died, Russian nobles met to name a new ruler. They chose Michael Romanov, the

grandnephew of Ivan the Terrible's wife. He began the Romanov dynasty, which ruled Russia for about 300 years.

1. What good and bad did Ivan the Terrible do?

_____

_____

PETER THE GREAT COMES TO POWER
Who was Peter the Great?

The Romanovs restored order to Russia. In the late 1600s, Peter I came to power. He was called **Peter the Great** because he was one of Russia's greatest reformers. He began an intense program of trying to modernize Russia. He also continued the trend of increasing the czar's power.

Lesson 4, *continued*

When Peter came to power, Russia was still a land of boyars and serfs. Serfdom lasted much longer in Russia than it did in western Europe. It continued into the mid-1800s.

When a Russian landowner sold a piece of land, he sold the serfs with it. Landowners could give away serfs as presents or to pay debts. It was also against the law for serfs to run away from their owners.

Most boyars knew little of western Europe. But Peter admired the nations of western Europe. He traveled in Europe to learn about new technology and ways of working. It was the first time a czar traveled in the West.

2. Why did Peter the Great visit Europe?

_____

_____

PETER RULES ABSOLUTELY
What changes did Peter the Great make?

Peter the Great wanted Russia to be the equal of the countries of western Europe. He wanted Russia to be strong both in its military and in its trade.

To meet these goals, Peter changed Russia. His first steps were to increase his powers, so he could force people to make the changes he wanted. He put the Russian Orthodox Church under his control. He reduced the power of nobles. He built up the army and made it better trained.

Peter also changed Russia through **westernization**. He took several steps to make Russia more western. He brought in potatoes as a new food, began Russia's first newspaper, gave more social status to women, and told the nobles to adopt Western clothes. He promoted education.

Peter also knew Russia needed a seaport that would make it easier to travel to the west. He fought a long war with Sweden to gain land along the shores of the Baltic Sea. There he built a grand new capital city, St. Petersburg. By the time of Peter's death in 1725, Russia was an important power in Europe.

3. How did Peter the Great increase his power?

_____

_____

Lesson 4, *continued*

As you read this lesson, complete the chart by explaining how Peter the Great solved each problem he encountered in his efforts to westernize Russia.

Problems	Solutions
1. Russian people did not believe that change was necessary.	
2. The Russian Orthodox Church was too strong.	
3. The great landowners had too much power.	
4. The Russian army was untrained and its tactics and weapons outdated.	
5. Russian society had to change to compete with the modern states of Europe.	
6. To promote education and growth, Russia needed a seaport for travel to the West.	
7. The port needed to be built.	
8. The new city needed to be settled.	

Guided Reading Workbook

Absolute Monarchs in Europe

Parliament Limits the English Monarchy

Key Terms and People

Charles I king of England who was executed

English Civil War war fought from 1642 to 1649 between the Royalists, or Cavaliers, and the Puritan supporters of Parliament

Oliver Cromwell leader of the Puritans

Restoration period after the monarchy was restored in England

habeas corpus law giving prisoners the right to obtain a document saying that the prisoner cannot go to jail without being brought before a judge

Glorious Revolution bloodless overthrow of King James II

constitutional monarchy government in which laws limit the monarch's power

cabinet group of government ministers that was a link between the monarch and Parliament

Before You Read

In the last lesson, you saw how power was becoming more absolute in Russia.

In this lesson, you will see how the power of the monarch was challenged and weakened in England.

As You Read

Use a diagram to take notes on each ruler's relationship with Parliament.

MONARCHS DEFY PARLIAMENT
***Why* was there tension between the monarchy and Parliament?**

When Queen Elizabeth I died, her cousin James, king of Scotland, became king of England. The reign of James I began a long series of struggles between king and Parliament. They fought over money. James's religious policies also angered the Puritans in Parliament.

During the reign of his son, **Charles I**, there was continued conflict between king and Parliament. Parliament forced Charles to sign the Petition of Right in 1628. By signing, Charles agreed that the king had to answer to Parliament. But he then dissolved Parliament and tried to raise money without it.

1. How did Charles I make Parliament angry?

_____

_____

Lesson 5, *continued*

ENGLISH CIVIL WAR
Who fought the English Civil War?

When Charles tried to force the Presbyterian Scots to follow the Anglican Church, Scotland threatened to invade England. When Charles called a new Parliament to get money to fight, it quickly passed laws to limit his power.

Soon England was fighting a civil war. Charles and his Royalists were opposed by the supporters of Parliament. Many of Parliament's supporters were Puritans.

The **English Civil War** lasted from 1642 to 1649. Under the leadership of **Oliver Cromwell**, the forces of the Puritans won. They tried and executed Charles for treason against Parliament. This was the first time a king had faced a public trial and execution. Cromwell crushed a rebellion in Ireland and tried to reform society at home. His government drafted the first constitution in modern Europe.

2. What happened as a result of the English Civil War?

_____

_____

RESTORATION AND REVOLUTION
What was the Restoration?

Soon after Cromwell's death, the government collapsed. Parliament asked Charles's older son to restore the monarchy. Charles II's rule, beginning in 1660, is called the **Restoration**.

Charles II's reign was calm. Parliament passed an important guarantee called *habeas corpus*. It gave all prisoners the right to have a judge decide whether they would be tried or set free. This kept monarchs from putting people in jail just for opposing them.

After Charles II's death in 1685, his brother became King James II. His pro-Catholic policies angered the English. They feared that he would restore Catholicism. In 1688, seven members of Parliament contacted James's older daughter, Mary, and her husband, William of Orange, prince of the Netherlands. Both were Protestants. The members wanted William and Mary to replace James II on the throne. James was forced to flee to France. When that took place, the bloodless revolution was called the **Glorious Revolution**.

3. Why did the Glorious Revolution take place?

_____

_____

LIMITS ON MONARCHS' POWER
How was the power of the monarchy decreased in England?

William and Mary agreed to rule according to the laws made by Parliament. England was now a **constitutional monarchy**, where laws limited the ruler's power.

William and Mary also agreed to accept the Bill of Rights. It guaranteed the people and Parliament certain rights.

By the 1700s, the government was often coming to a standstill when the monarch and Parliament disagreed. This led to the development of the **cabinet**. This group of government ministers became the first link between the monarch and Parliament.

4. What three changes gave Parliament more power in England?

_____

_____

As you read, take notes to fill in the diagram describing relations
between Parliament and each English ruler listed.

```
┌──────────────────────────────────────────────────────┐
│ 1. King James I                                      │
│    (1603–1625)                                       │
│                                                      │
│                                                      │
│                                                      │
│                                                      │
└──────────────────────────────────────────────────────┘
                          │
                          ▼
┌──────────────────────────────────────────────────────┐
│ 2. Charles I                                         │
│    (1625–1649)                                       │
│                                                      │
│                                                      │
│                                                      │
│                                                      │
└──────────────────────────────────────────────────────┘
                          │
                          ▼
┌──────────────────────────────────────────────────────┐
│ 3. Oliver Cromwell                                   │
│    (1649–1658)                                       │
│                                                      │
│                                                      │
│                                                      │
│                                                      │
└──────────────────────────────────────────────────────┘
                          │
                          ▼
┌──────────────────────────────────────────────────────┐
│ 4. Charles II                                        │
│    (1660–1685)                                       │
│                                                      │
│                                                      │
│                                                      │
│                                                      │
└──────────────────────────────────────────────────────┘
                          │
                          ▼
┌──────────────────────────────────────────────────────┐
│ 5. James II                                          │
│    (1685–1688)                                       │
│                                                      │
│                                                      │
│                                                      │
│                                                      │
└──────────────────────────────────────────────────────┘
                          │
                          ▼
┌──────────────────────────────────────────────────────┐
│ 6. William and Mary                                  │
│    (1689–1702)                                       │
│                                                      │
│                                                      │
│                                                      │
│                                                      │
└──────────────────────────────────────────────────────┘
```

Enlightenment and Revolution

The Scientific Revolution

Key Terms and People

geocentric theory in the Middle Ages, view which held that the earth was an immovable object located at the center of the universe

Scientific Revolution new way of thinking about the natural world based on careful observation and the questioning of accepted beliefs

heliocentric theory idea that the earth and the other planets revolve around the sun

Galileo Galilei Italian scientist who invented the first working telescope; his discoveries put him into conflict with the Roman Catholic Church

scientific method logical procedure for gathering information and testing ideas

Isaac Newton English scientist who discovered laws of motion and gravity

deism Enlightenment belief that God created the universe and then allowed it to run on its own following natural laws

Before You Read

In the last lesson, you read about how Parliament limited the English monarchy.

In this lesson, you will read about how the Enlightenment transformed Europe and helped lead to the American Revolution.

As You Read

Use a chart to record developments in the Scientific Revolution.

THE ROOTS OF MODERN SCIENCE
How did modern science begin?

During the Middle Ages, few scholars questioned beliefs that had been long held. Europeans based their ideas on what ancient Greeks and Romans believed, or on the Bible. People still thought that the earth was the center of the universe. They believed that the sun, moon, other planets, and stars moved around it. This is known as the **geocentric theory**.

In the mid-1500s, attitudes began to change. Scholars started what is called the **Scientific Revolution**. It was a new way of thinking about the natural world. It was based on careful observation and the willingness to question old beliefs. European voyages of exploration helped to bring about the Scientific Revolution.

1. What was the Scientific Revolution?

_____

_____

A REVOLUTIONARY MODEL OF THE UNIVERSE; THE SCIENTIFIC METHOD
How did new ideas change accepted thinking in astronomy?

The first challenge to accepted thinking in science came in astronomy. In the early 1500s, Nicolaus Copernicus, a Polish astronomer, studied the stars and planets. He developed a **heliocentric theory**. Heliocentric means sun-centered. It said that Earth, like all the other planets, revolved around the sun. This went against the geocentric theory that the earth was at the center of the universe. In the early 1600s, Johannes Kepler used mathematics to prove that Copernicus's basic idea was correct.

An Italian scientist, **Galileo Galilei**, made several discoveries that also undercut ancient ideas. He made an early telescope and used it to study the planets. He found that Jupiter had moons, the sun had spots, and Earth's moon was rough. Catholic Church authorities forced Galileo to take back his statements. Still, his ideas spread.

Interest in science led to a new approach, the **scientific method**. With this method, scientists ask a question, then form a hypothesis, or an attempt to answer the question. Then they test the hypothesis. Finally, they change the hypothesis if needed.

The English writer Francis Bacon helped create this new approach to knowledge. He said scientists should base their thinking on what they can observe and test. The French mathematician René Descartes also influenced the use of the scientific method. His thinking was based on logic and mathematics.

2. What old belief about the universe did the new discoveries destroy?

_____

_____

NEWTON EXPLAINS THE LAW OF GRAVITY; THE SCIENTIFIC REVOLUTION SPREADS
What scientific discoveries were made?

In the mid-1600s, the English scientist **Isaac Newton** described the law of gravity. Using mathematics, Newton showed that the same force ruled both the motion of planets and the action of bodies on the earth. He believed that God created the universe and then such natural forces took over. This belief is called **deism**.

Other scientists made new tools to study the world around them. One invented a microscope.

Doctors also made advances. One made drawings that showed the different parts of the human body. Another learned how the heart pumped blood through the body. In the late 1700s, Edward Jenner first used the process called vaccination to prevent smallpox disease.

Scientists made progress in chemistry as well. Robert Boyle questioned the old idea that things were made of only four elements—earth, air, fire, and water. He believed that the physical world was made up of smaller components that joined together.

3. How did the science of medicine change?

_____

_____

Lesson 1, *continued*

As you read about the revolution in scientific thinking, take notes to answer the questions.

How did the following help pave the way for the Scientific Revolution?
1. The Renaissance
2. Age of European exploration

What did each scientist discover about the universe?
3. Nicolaus Copernicus
4. Johannes Kepler
5. Galileo Galilei
6. Isaac Newton

What important developments took place in the following areas?
7. Scientific instruments
8. Medicine
9. Chemistry

Enlightenment and Revolution

Enlightenment Thinkers

Key Terms and People

Enlightenment 18th-century European movement in which thinkers attempted to apply the principles of reason and the scientific method to all aspects of society

social contract agreement by which people define and limit their individual rights, thus creating an organized society or government

John Locke English philosopher and founder of British empiricism; he developed political and economic theories during the Enlightenment. He declared that people have a right to rebel against governments that do not protect their rights.

philosophe one of a group of social thinkers in France during the Enlightenment

rationalism belief that truth could be found through reason or logical thinking

Voltaire French philosopher and author who believed in tolerance, reason, freedom of religious belief, and freedom of speech

Montesquieu French political philosopher who explored democratic theories of government; he proposed a government divided into three branches and greatly influenced the United States Constitution.

Rousseau Swiss-French political philosopher; he championed the freedom of the individual and the notion that all people were equal.

Before You Read

In the last lesson, you read about how the Scientific Revolution began in Europe.

In this lesson, you will read about how the Enlightenment began in Europe.

As You Read

Use a web diagram to summarize the ideas of different Enlightenment thinkers.

TWO VIEWS ON GOVERNMENT
What were the views of Hobbes and Locke?

The **Enlightenment** was an intellectual movement. Enlightenment thinkers tried to apply reason and the scientific method to laws that shaped human actions. They hoped to build a society founded on ideas of the Scientific Revolution. Two English writers—Thomas Hobbes and John Locke—were important to this movement. They came to very different conclusions about government and human nature.

Hobbes wrote that there would be a war of "every man against every man" if

Lesson 2, *continued*

there were no government. To avoid this war, Hobbes said, people formed a **social contract**. It was an agreement between people and their government. People gave up their rights to the government so they could live in a safe and orderly way. The best government, he said, is that of a strong king who can force all people to obey.

John Locke believed that people have three natural rights. They are life, liberty, and property. The purpose of government is to protect these rights. When it fails to do so, he said, people have a right to overthrow the government.

1. How were Hobbes's and Locke's views different?

   _____

   _____

   _____

THE PHILOSOPHES ADVOCATE REASON
Who were the philosophes?

French thinkers, called **philosophes**, had five main beliefs: (1) thinkers can find the truth by using reason—this is known as **rationalism**; (2) what is natural is good and reasonable, and human actions are shaped by natural laws; (3) acting according to nature can bring happiness; (4) by taking a scientific view, people and society can make progress and advance to a better life; and (5) by using reason, people can gain freedom.

The most brilliant of the philosophes was the writer **Voltaire**. He fought for tolerance, reason, freedom of religious belief, and freedom of speech. Baron de **Montesquieu** wrote about political freedom and separation of powers— dividing power among the separate branches of government. The third great philosophe was Jean Jacques **Rousseau**. He wrote in favor of human freedom. Rousseau believed that all people were naturally free and good but that civilization chained them. He wanted a true democracy in which all people were equal, and government was guided by the "general will" of the people. Cesare Beccaria was an Italian philosophe. He spoke out against abuses of justice and in favor of all people's rights. He believed that laws should be based on fairness and reason.

2. Name the types of freedoms that Enlightenment thinkers championed.

   _____

   _____

Lesson 2, *continued*

As you read, fill in the diagram by describing the beliefs of
Enlightenment thinkers and writers.

| 1. Voltaire | 2. Montesquieu |

Enlightenment Philosophers and Writers

| 3. Jean Jacques Rousseau | 4. Cesare Bonesana Beccari |

Enlightenment and Revolution

The Enlightenment Spreads

Key Terms and People

salons social gatherings for discussing ideas and enjoying art

baroque grand, ornate style in arts and architecture in the 1600s and early 1700s

neoclassical simple, elegant style in 1700s, inspired by ancient Greece and Rome

Mary Wollstonecraft argued for greater education opportunities for women and urged women to enter the male-dominated fields of medicine and politics

enlightened despot one of the 18th-century European monarchs who was inspired by Enlightenment ideas to rule fairly and respect the rights of subjects

Catherine the Great Czarina of Russia who took steps to reform and modernize Russia

Before You Read

In the last lesson, you read about how Enlightenment ideas began.

In this lesson, you will read about the spread of these ideas.

As You Read

Use a chart to take notes on people who spread Enlightenment ideas.

A WORLD OF IDEAS
How did ideas spread from individual to individual?

In the 1700s, people came to Paris to hear the ideas of the Enlightenment. Writers and artists held social gatherings called **salons**. A woman named Marie-Thérèse Geoffrin became famous for hosting these discussions.

With her funds, Denis Diderot and other thinkers wrote and published a huge set of books called the *Encyclopedia*. Their aim was to gather all that was known about the world. The French government and Catholic Church banned the books at first. They did not like many of the ideas in them. Later, however, they changed their minds.

The ideas of the Enlightenment were spread throughout Europe by works like the *Encyclopedia* and through meetings in homes. The ideas also spread to the growing middle class. This group was becoming wealthy but had less social status than nobles. They also had very little political power. Ideas about equality sounded good to them.

1. Why were salons important?

_____

_____

NEW ARTISTIC STYLES; WOMEN AND THE ENLIGHTENMENT
How were ideas about women changing?

The arts—painting, architecture, music, and literature—moved in new directions in the late 1700s. They used Enlightenment ideas of order and reason.

Earlier European painting had been very grand and highly decorated. It was a style known as **baroque**. A new elegant style of painting and architecture developed. This style borrowed ideas and themes from ancient Greece and Rome. This was called **neoclassical**.

In music, the style of the period is called classical. Franz Joseph Haydn, Wolfgang Amadeus Mozart, and Ludwig von Beethoven composed music that was elegant and original. In literature, the novel form became popular with the middle class.

Many male Enlightenment thinkers held traditional views about women's roles. Others argued for more education and equality. Women also wrote in protest of their lack of equality. Mary Astell, an English writer, protested the unequal relationship between man and woman in marriage. **Mary Wollstonecraft** argued that a woman's education should be equal to a man's. She believed women should enter the fields of medicine and politics.

2. What kind of equality were women seeking during the Enlightenment?

    _____

    _____

ENLIGHTENMENT AND MONARCHY; LEGACY OF THE ENLIGHTENMENT
What were Enlightenment views about individuals?

Some Enlightenment thinkers believed that the best form of government was a monarchy. Rulers who followed Enlightenment ideas in part but were unwilling to give up much power were called **enlightened despots**.

Frederick the Great of Prussia was an enlightened despot. He allowed religious freedom, improved schooling, and reformed the justice system. Joseph II of Austria ended serfdom, which made peasants slaves to land-owning nobles. This reform was later undone.

Catherine the Great of Russia was a ruler also influenced by Enlightenment ideas. She had hoped to end serfdom. But after a bloody peasant revolt, she gave the nobles even more power over serfs. Catherine did manage to gain new land for Russia when Russia, Prussia, and Austria agreed to divide Poland.

Enlightenment writers questioned the divine right of monarchs, the union of church and state, and the existence of unequal social classes. As a result, Enlightenment ideas strongly influenced the American and French revolutions. Enlightenment thinkers helped spread the idea of scientific and social progress. By using reason, they said, society can be improved. Enlightenment thinkers helped make the world less religious and more worldly. They also stressed the importance of the individual.

3. Explain the influence of Enlightenment ideas.

    _____

    _____

Name _____ Class _____ Date _____

As you read about the spread of ideas during the Age of Reason, explain how each of the following people reflected Enlightenment ideas.

1. Mary Astell	
2. Mary Wollstonecraft	
3. Frederick the Great	
4. Joseph II	
5. Catherine the Great	

Guided Reading Workbook

The American Revolution

Key Terms and People

Declaration of Independence document declaring American independence from Britain and the reasons for it.

Thomas Jefferson American statesman; third president of the United States; author of the Declaration of Independence and one of its signers.

checks and balances system in which each branch of government checks, or limits, the power of the other two branches.

federal system system of government in which power is divided between the national and state governments.

Bill of Rights first ten amendments to the U.S. Constitution, which protect citizens' basic rights and freedoms.

Before You Read

In the last lesson, you read about the spread of Enlightenment ideas in Europe.

In this lesson, you will read about how Enlightenment ideas influenced the American Revolution.

As You Read

Use a chart to list the causes and effects of the American Revolution.

BRITAIN AND ITS AMERICAN COLONIES
How were the colonies governed?

The British colonies in North America grew in population and wealth during the 1700s. Population went from about 250,000 in 1700 to 2,150,000 in 1770. Economically, they prospered on trade with the nations of Europe. The 13 colonies also had a kind of self-government. People in the colonies began to see themselves less and less as British subjects. Still, Parliament passed laws that governed the colonies. One set of laws banned trade with any nation other than Britain.

1. How did the colonists' image of themselves clash with their status as colonists?

_____

_____

AMERICANS WIN INDEPENDENCE
What caused Britain and America to grow apart?

The high cost of the French and Indian War led Parliament to tax the colonists. The colonists became very angry. They had never before paid taxes directly to the British government. They said that the taxes violated their rights. Since Parliament had no members from the colonies, they said, Parliament had no right to tax them.

The colonists met the first tax, passed in 1765, with a boycott of British goods. Their refusal to buy British products was very effective. It forced Parliament to repeal the law.

Over the next decade, the colonists and Britain grew further apart. Some colonists wanted to push the colonies to independence. They took actions that caused Britain to act harshly. Eventually, the conflict led to war. Representatives of the colonies met in a congress and formed an army. In July 1776, they announced that they were independent of Britain. They issued the **Declaration of Independence**. It was based on Enlightenment ideas. **Thomas Jefferson** wrote it.

From 1775 to 1781, the colonies and the British fought a war in North America. The colonists had a poorly equipped army, and Britain was one of the most powerful nations in the world. However, in the end, the colonies won their independence.

The British people grew tired of the cost of the war and pushed Parliament to agree to a peace. The Americans were also helped greatly by aid from France. In 1783, the two sides signed a treaty. In it, Britain recognized the independent United States of America.

2. Name some of the steps that led to the American Revolution.

_____

_____

AMERICANS CREATE A REPUBLIC
What are some fundamental ideas in the U.S. Constitution?

The 13 states formed a new government under the Article of Confederation. This government was very weak. States held all the power, and the central government had little. This proved unworkable. In 1787, American leaders met again. They wrote a new framework of government.

The Constitution of the United States drew on many Enlightenment ideas. It used Montesquieu's idea of separation of powers into three branches of government. Through a system of **checks and balances**, each branch was able to prevent other branches from abusing their power. The Constitution also set up a **federal system**. Under this system, power was divided between national and state governments.

The Constitution also used Locke's idea of putting power in the hands of the people. It used Voltaire's ideas to protect the right to free speech and freedom of religion. It used Beccaria's ideas about a fair system of justice.

Many of these rights were ensured in a set of additions to the Constitution called the **Bill of Rights**. The inclusion of a bill of rights helped win approval for the Constitution.

3. Explain how the Constitution divides power.

_____

_____

Lesson 4, *continued*

As you read, note some causes and effects relating to the American Revolution and the establishment of the United States as a republic.

Causes	Events	Effects
	1. British Parliament passes Stamp Act.	
	2. British close Boston's harbor and station troops in city.	
	3. Second Continental Congress votes to form an army under command of George Washington.	
	4. France enters the war in 1778.	
	5. By approving the Articles of Confederation, states create a weak national government.	

Guided Reading Workbook

The French Revolution and Napoleon

The French Revolution Begins

Key Terms and People

Old Regime system of feudalism

estate social class of people

Louis XVI weak king who came to French throne in 1774

Marie Antoinette unpopular queen; wife of Louis XVI

Estates-General assembly of representatives from all three estates

National Assembly French congress established by representatives of the Third Estate

Tennis Court Oath promise made by Third Estate representatives to draw up a new constitution

Great Fear wave of panic

Before You Read

In the last lesson, you read about the Enlightenment and the American Revolution.

In this lesson, you will learn about the beginning of the French Revolution.

As You Read

Use a chart to take notes on the causes and effects of the early stages of the French Revolution.

THE OLD ORDER
How was French society unequal?

In the 1700s, France was the leading country of Europe. However, beneath the surface there were major problems.

A political and social system called the **Old Regime** remained in place. The French were divided into three classes, or **estates.** The First Estate consisted of the Roman Catholic clergy. The Second Estate was made up of nobles. Only about two percent of the people belonged to these two estates. Yet they owned 20 percent of the land.

Everybody else belonged to the Third Estate. This huge group included the bourgeoisie—merchants and skilled workers—city workers, and peasants.

Members of the Third Estate had few rights. They paid up to half of their income in taxes, while the rich paid almost none.

1. What were the three classes of French society?

_____

_____

THE FORCES OF CHANGE
Why were the French ready for the revolution?

Three factors led to revolution. First, the Enlightenment spread the idea that everyone should be equal. The powerless people in the Third Estate liked this idea. Second, the French economy was failing. High taxes kept profits low, and food supplies were short. The government owed money. Third, King **Louis XVI** was a weak leader. His wife, **Marie Antoinette,** was unpopular. She was from Austria, France's long-time enemy, and was known for her extravagant spending.

In the 1780s, France was deep in debt. Louis tried to tax the nobles. Instead, they forced the king to call a meeting of the **Estates-General,** an assembly of delegates of the three estates.

2. What three factors led to revolution?

_____

_____

DAWN OF THE REVOLUTION
How did the Revolution begin?

The meeting of the Estates-General began in May 1789 with arguments over how to count votes. In the past, each estate would cast one vote. The Third Estate now wanted each delegate to have a vote. The king and the other estates did not agree to the plan because the Third Estate was larger and would have more votes.

The Third Estate then broke with the others and met separately. In June 1789, its delegates voted to rename themselves the **National Assembly.** They claimed to represent all the people. This was the beginning of representative government in France.

At one point, the members of the Third Estate were locked out of their meeting room. They broke down a door leading to a tennis court. Then they promised to stay there until they made a new constitution. This promise was called the **Tennis Court Oath.**

Louis tried to make peace. He ordered the clergy and nobles to join the National Assembly. However, trouble erupted. Rumors spread that foreign soldiers were going to attack French citizens. On July 14, an angry crowd captured the Bastille, a Paris prison. The mob wanted to get gunpowder for their weapons in order to defend the city.

3. Why did the National Assembly form?

_____

_____

A GREAT FEAR SWEEPS FRANCE
What was the Great Fear?

A wave of violence called the **Great Fear** swept the country. Peasants broke into and burned nobles' houses. They tore up documents that had forced them to pay fees to the nobles. Late in 1789, a mob of women marched from Paris to the king's palace at Versailles. They were angry about high bread prices and demanded that the king come to Paris. They hoped he would end hunger in the city. The king and queen left Versailles, never to return.

4. Who led the events that happened during the Great Fear?

_____

_____

Name _____ Class _____ Date _____

Lesson 1, *continued*

As you read about the dawn of revolution in France, write notes to answer questions about the causes of the French Revolution.

How did each of the following contribute to the revolutionary mood in France?	
1. The three estates	2. Enlightenment ideas
3. Economic crisis	4. Weak leadership

How did each of the following events lead to the French Revolution?	
5. Meeting of the Estates-General	6. Establishment of the National Assembly
7. Tennis Court Oath	8. Storming of the Bastille

Guided Reading Workbook

The French Revolution and Napoleon

Revolution Brings Reform and Terror

Key Terms and People

Legislative Assembly assembly that replaced the National Assembly in 1791

émigré noble or other person who left France during the peasant uprisings and who hoped to come back to restore the old system

sans-culotte radical group of Parisian wage-earners

Jacobin member of the Jacobin Club, a radical political organization

guillotine machine for beheading people

Maximilien Robespierre revolutionary leader who tried to wipe out every trace of France's past monarchy and nobility

Reign of Terror period of Robespierre's rule

Before You Read

In the last lesson, you read how the French Revolution began.

In this lesson, you will learn what happened during the revolution.

As You Read

Use a timeline to identify the major events that followed the creation of the Constitution of 1791.

THE ASSEMBLY REFORMS FRANCE

What reforms resulted from the revolution?

In August 1789, the National Assembly took steps to change France. One new law ended all the special rights that members of the First Estate and Second Estate had enjoyed. Another law gave French men equal rights. Though women did not get these rights, it was a bold step. Other laws gave the state power over the Catholic Church.

Catholic peasants remained loyal to the Church. They were angry that the Church would be part of the state.

Thereafter, many of them opposed the Revolution's reforms.

For months, the assembly worked on plans for a new government. During this time, Louis was fearful for his safety. One night, he and his family tried to escape the country. They were caught, brought back to Paris, and watched by guards. This escape attempt made the king and queen even more unpopular. It also increased the power of his enemies.

1. What new laws came into being?

_____

_____

Lesson 2, *continued*

DIVISIONS DEVELOP
What groups called for different kinds of changes?

In the fall of 1791, the assembly finished its new constitution. It took away most of the king's power. The assembly then turned over its power to a new assembly, the **Legislative Assembly.**

This new assembly soon divided into groups. Radicals wanted to make many changes in the way government was run. Moderates wanted only some changes in government. Conservatives didn't mind having a limited monarchy and wanted few changes in government.

Groups outside the Assembly wanted to influence the government, too. One group wanted to return to the old ways, before the Revolution. This group included the **émigrés,** nobles and others who had fled France earlier. Another group wanted even greater changes. This group included the **sans-culottes.** These wage earners and small shopkeepers wanted a greater voice in government.

2. In what ways did the émigrés and sans-culottes have opposite goals?

_____

_____

WAR AND EXECUTION
What caused the French people to take extreme measures?

At the same time, France faced serious trouble on its borders. Kings in other countries feared that their people would revolt, too. They wanted to use force to give control of France back to Louis XVI. Soon, foreign soldiers were marching toward Paris. Many people thought that the king and queen were ready to help the enemy. Angry French citizens imprisoned them. Many nobles, priests, and other supporters of the royalty were killed by the peasants.

The government took strong steps to reduce the danger of foreign troops. It took away all the king's powers. In 1792, the National Convention—another new government—was formed. **Jacobins,** members of a radical political club, soon took control of this new government. They declared Louis a common citizen. He was then tried for treason and convicted. Like many others, the king was beheaded by a machine called the **guillotine.** The National Convention also ordered thousands of French people into the army.

3. What happened to the king?

_____

_____

THE TERROR GRIPS FRANCE; END OF THE TERROR
What was the Reign of Terror?

Maximilien Robespierre became leader of France. He headed the Committee of Public Safety. It tried and put to death "enemies of the Revolution." Thousands were killed. Robespierre's rule, which began in 1793, was called the **Reign of Terror.** It ended in July 1794, when Robespierre himself was put to death.

The French people were tired of the killing and the unrest. They wanted a return to order. Moderate leaders drafted a new, less revolutionary plan of government.

4. How long did the Reign of Terror last?

_____

_____

Guided Reading Workbook

Lesson 2, *continued*

As you read about the events of the French Revolution, answer the
questions about the time line.

1789 Aug.	**National Assembly adopts Declaration of the Rights of Man.**	1. What are some rights this document guarantees French citizens?
1790	**National Assembly reforms status of church.**	2. What caused the peasants to oppose many of these reforms?
1791 Sep.	**National Assembly hands power to Legislative Assembly**	3. What political factions made up the Legislative Assembly?
1792 April	**Legislative Assembly declares war on Austria.**	4. What did European monarchs fear from France?
Aug.	**Parisians invade Tuileries and imprison royal family.**	
Sep.	**Parisian mobs massacre more than 1,000 prisoners.**	
1793 Jan.	**Ex-king Louis XVI is executed.**	5. What effects did the September Massacres have on the government?
July	**Robespierre leads Committee of Public Safety; Reign of Terror begins.**	
1794 July	**Robespierre is executed; Reign of Terror ends.**	6. What was the stated aim of Robespierre and his supporters?
1795	**National Convention adopts new constitution.**	7. What were some consequences of the Reign of Terror?

The French Revolution and Napoleon

Napoleon's Empire

Key Terms and People

Napoleon Bonaparte military leader who seized power in France

coup d'état sudden takeover of a government

plebiscite vote by the people

lycée government-run public school

concordat agreement

Napoleonic Code complete set of laws set up by Napoleon that eliminated many injustices

Battle of Trafalgar British defeat of Napoleon's forces at sea

blockade forced closing of ports

Continental System Napoleon's policy of preventing trade and communication between Great Britain and other European nations

guerrilla Spanish peasant fighter

Peninsular War war that Napoleon fought in Spain

scorched-earth policy policy of burning fields and slaughtering livestock so that enemy troops would find nothing to eat

Waterloo battle in Belgium that was Napoleon's final defeat

Hundred Days Napoleon's last bid for power, which ended at Waterloo

Before You Read

In the last lesson, you read about the Revolution's extremes, including the Reign of Terror.

In this lesson, you will learn how Napoleon grabbed power and brought order to France.

As You Read

Use a chart to analyze the goals and results of Napoleon's actions as emperor of France.

NAPOLEON SEIZES POWER; NAPOLEON RULES FRANCE

How did Napoleon rise to power?

In 1795, **Napoleon Bonaparte** led soldiers against French royalists who were attacking the National Convention. Napoleon used troops to take control of the French government. This was a **coup d'état,** or a sudden takeover of power. Napoleon held the powers of a dictator.

In 1800, a **plebiscite,** or vote of the people, approved a new constitution. Napoleon took power as first consul. He started **lycées**—new public schools for ordinary male citizens. He signed a **concordat,** or agreement, with the pope. This gave the Church back some power.

He wrote a new set of laws, called the **Napoleonic Code,** which gave all French citizens the same rights. However, the new laws took away many individual rights won during the Revolution. For example, they limited free speech and restored slavery in French colonies.

1. What was the Napoleonic Code?

_____

_____

NAPOLEON CREATES AN EMPIRE; NAPOLEON'S COSTLY MISTAKES
What mistakes did Napoleon make abroad?

Napoleon had hoped to make his empire larger in both Europe and the New World. Napoleon's only loss during this time was to the British navy in the **Battle of Trafalgar.**

Napoleon loved power. But his empire fell because he made three big mistakes.

His first mistake was caused by his desire to crush Britain's economy. In 1806, he ordered a **blockade** and stopped all trade between Britain and other European nations. Napoleon called this policy the **Continental System.** It was to make continental Europe self-sufficient. It did not work as planned. Soon the French economy, along with others on the European continent, weakened.

Napoleon's second mistake was to make his brother king of Spain in 1808. With help from Britain, groups of Spanish peasant fighters called **guerrillas** fought Napoleon for five years.

Napoleon lost 300,000 troops during this **Peninsular War.**

Napoleon's third mistake was perhaps his worst. In 1812, he tried to conquer Russia. As the Russians retreated, however, they followed a **scorched-earth policy.** They burned their fields and killed their livestock so Napoleon's armies could not eat what they left behind. Thousands of soldiers died from the bitter cold and hunger on their way home. Others deserted. Napoleon entered Russia with more than 420,000 soldiers but left with only 10,000.

2. What happened to Napoleon's soldiers in Russia?

_____

_____

NAPOLEON'S DOWNFALL
How was Napoleon defeated?

Britain, Russia, Prussia, Sweden, and Austria joined forces and attacked France. In 1814, Napoleon gave up his throne and was sent away to the tiny island of Elba off the Italian coast.

In March 1815, Napoleon escaped from Elba and returned to France. He took power and raised another army.

The rest of the European powers raised armies to fight against Napoleon. They defeated Napoleon in his final battle near a Belgian town called **Waterloo.** This defeat ended Napoleon's last attempt at power, which was called the **Hundred Days.** He was then sent to a far-off island in the southern Atlantic Ocean. He died there in 1821.

3. What was Napoleon's last attempt at power, and where did it end?

_____

_____

As you read about Napoleon, note the goals and results of some of his actions.

Actions	Goal(s)	Result(s)
1. Establishment of national bank and efficient tax-collection system		
2. Enacting Napoleonic Code of law		
3. Sending troops to Saint Domingue		
4. Selling Louisiana Territory to the United States		
5. Waging Battle of Trafalgar		

The French Revolution and Napoleon

Lesson 4

The Congress of Vienna

Key Terms and People

Congress of Vienna meetings in Vienna for the purpose of restoring order to Europe

Klemens von Metternich key leader at the Congress of Vienna

balance of power condition in which no one country becomes a threat to another

legitimacy bringing back to power the kings that Napoleon had driven out

Holy Alliance league formed by Russia, Austria, and Prussia

Concert of Europe series of alliances to help prevent revolution

Before You Read

In the last lesson, you saw how Napoleon's empire collapsed.

In this lesson, you will learn how the rest of Europe reacted to both the French Revolution and Napoleon's rise and fall.

As You Read

Use a chart to take notes on the goals and outcomes of the Congress of Vienna.

METTERNICH'S PLAN FOR EUROPE
What **was the Congress of Vienna?**

In 1814, leaders of many nations met to draw up a peace plan for Europe. This series of meetings was called the **Congress of Vienna.** The most important person at the Congress of Vienna was the foreign minister of Austria, **Klemens von Metternich.** He developed the peace conditions that were finally accepted.

Metternich had three goals at the congress. First, he wanted the countries around France to be stronger. This would make sure that the French could not attack another country again.

Second, he wanted a **balance of power** in which no one nation was strong enough to threaten other nations. Third, he wanted **legitimacy.** This meant restoring monarchs to the thrones they had had before Napoleon's conquests. The other leaders agreed with Metternich's ideas.

Metternich achieved his first goal when the congress strengthened the small nations that surrounded France. Meanwhile, France was not punished too severely. It remained independent and was allowed to keep some overseas possessions. This helped achieve Metternich's second goal to create a balance of power.

The congress also worked to fulfill Metternich's third goal. Many rulers were returned to power in states throughout Europe, including France.

The Congress of Vienna created very successful peace agreements. None of the great powers fought against one another for 40 years. Some did not fight in a war for the rest of the century.

1. What three goals did Metternich have?

_____

_____

POLITICAL CHANGES BEYOND VIENNA
How did European leaders respond to the effects of the French Revolution?

Many European rulers were nervous about the effects of the French Revolution. In 1815, Czar Alexander of Russia, Emperor Francis I of Austria, and King Frederick William III of Prussia formed the **Holy Alliance.** Other alliances created by Metternich were called the **Concert of Europe.** The idea of these alliances was for nations to help one another if revolution came.

Across Europe, conservatives held control of European governments.

Conservatives were people who opposed the ideals of the French Revolution. They also usually supported the rights and powers of royalty. They did not encourage individual liberties. They did not want any calls for equal rights.

But many other people still believed in the ideals of the French Revolution. They thought that all people should be equal and share in power. Later they would again fight for these rights.

People in the Americas also felt the desire for freedom. Spanish colonies in the Americas revolted against the restored Spanish king. Many colonies won independence from Spain. National feeling grew in Europe, too. Soon, people in areas such as Italy, Germany, and Greece would rebel and form new nations. The French Revolution had changed the politics of Europe and beyond.

2. What happened to ideas about freedom and independence after the French Revolution?

_____

_____

Lesson 4, *continued*

As you read about the meeting of the Congress of Vienna, fill in the diagram below.

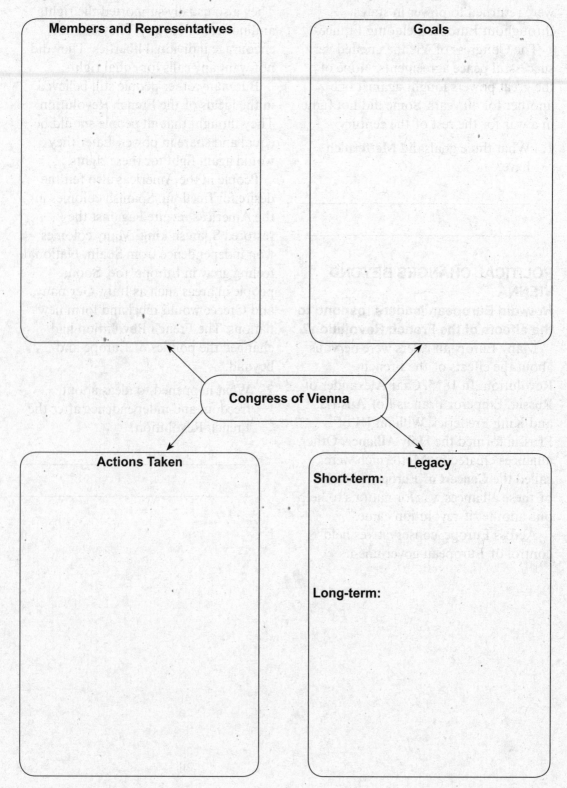

Members and Representatives

Goals

Congress of Vienna

Actions Taken

Legacy

Short-term:

Long-term:

Revolutions Sweep the West

Latin American Peoples Win Independence

Key Terms and People

peninsulare Latin American born in Spain

creole Spaniard born in Latin America

mulatto person of mixed European and African ancestry

Simón Bolívar leader of Venezuelan independence movement

José de San Martín leader who helped win independence for Chile and Argentina

Miguel Hidalgo priest who began the revolt against Spanish rule in Mexico

José María Morelos leader of the Mexican revolt after Hidalgo was defeated

Before You Read

In the last lesson, you read about revolution and the Congress of Vienna.

In this lesson, you will learn how Latin American countries became independent.

As You Read

Use a chart to identify details about Latin American independence movements.

COLONIAL SOCIETY DIVIDED
What classes existed in Latin American society?

In Latin America, society was divided into six classes of people. *Peninsulares*—those born in Spain—were at the top. Next were **creoles,** or Spaniards who had been born in Latin America. Below them were mestizos. Mestizos had mixed European and Indian ancestry. Next were **mulattos,** with mixed European and African ancestry, and then Africans. At the bottom were Indians.

1. Which groups of society were of European ancestry?

_____

_____

REVOLUTIONS IN THE AMERICAS
Where in Latin America was independence first declared?

In the late 1700s, colonial peoples in Latin America fought for independence. The French colony of Saint Domingue was the first Latin American colony to fight for independence.

Almost all of the people who lived in the French colony were slaves of African origin. In 1791, about 100,000 of them rose in revolt. Toussaint L'Ouverture, a former slave, became their leader. In 1802, Napoleon sent troops to the island to end the rebellion. They failed. In 1804, the colony declared its independence as Haiti.

2. How did Haiti become independent?

_____

_____

CREOLES LEAD INDEPENDENCE
Why **did creoles want independence?**

Creoles felt that they were not treated fairly. This bad feeling boiled over when Napoleon overthrew the king of Spain and named his own brother as king. Creoles in Latin America had no loyalty to the new king. They revolted. Even after the old king was restored, they did not give up their fight for freedom.

Two leaders pushed much of South America to independence. **Simón Bolívar** was a writer, fighter, and political thinker. He survived defeats and exile to help win independence for Venezuela in 1821. **José de San Martín** helped win independence for Argentina in 1816 and Chile in 1818. Bolívar led their combined armies to a great victory in 1824. This victory gained independence for all the Spanish colonies.

3. Which two great leaders led the fights for independence in Venezuela, Chile, and Argentina?

_____

MEXICO ENDS SPANISH RULE; BRAZIL'S ROYAL LIBERATOR
How **did Mexico and Brazil achieve independence?**

In Mexico, mestizos and Indians led the fight for independence. In 1810, **Miguel Hidalgo,** a village priest, called for a revolt against Spanish rule. Creoles united with the Spanish government to put down this revolt by the lower classes.

Hidalgo lost, but Padre **José María Morelos** took over leadership of the rebels. Fighting continued until 1815, when the creoles won.

After a revolution in Spain put a new government in power, the creoles joined with the other groups fighting for independence. In 1821, Mexico won its independence. In 1823, the region of Central America separated itself from Mexico.

In Brazil, 8,000 creoles signed a paper asking the son of Portugal's king to rule an independent Brazil. He agreed. Brazil became free that year through a bloodless revolt.

4. How were the drives for independence in Mexico and Brazil different?

_____

_____

Lesson 1, *continued*

As you read this lesson, fill out the chart below to help you better understand why and how Latin Americans fought colonial rule.

Independence for Haiti	
Reasons	**Strategy**
1. Why did slaves in the French colony of Saint Domingue revolt?	2. What events led up to General Dessalines's declaration of independence for Haiti?

South American Wars of Independence	
Reasons	**Strategy**
3. How did events in Europe lead to revolution in the Spanish colonies?	4. What tactics did José de San Martín and Simón Bolívar use to defeat Spanish forces in South America?

End of Spanish Rule in Mexico	
Reasons	**Strategy**
5. What is the significance of the *grito de Dolores*?	6. What role did Indians, mestizos, and creoles play in Mexico's independence from Spain?

Revolutions Sweep the West

Europe Faces Revolutions

Key Terms and People

conservative person who supported the monarchy

liberal person who wanted to give more power to elected legislatures

radical person who wanted to end the rule by kings and give full voting rights to all people

anarchism belief that government is harmful and not needed

nationalism belief that a person's loyalty belongs to the nation itself instead of to the nation's ruler

nation-state country with its own independent government

Balkans region including all or part of present-day Greece, Albania, Bulgaria, Romania, Turkey, and former Yugoslavia

Louis-Napoleon winner of the presidential election in France in 1848, later emperor

Alexander II ruler of Russia who freed the serfs

Before You Read

In the last lesson, you read about Latin American independence movements.

In this lesson, you will learn about revolutions in Europe.

As You Read

Use a chart to analyze the outcomes of revolutions in Europe.

CLASH OF PHILOSOPHIES; NATIONALISM DEVELOPS
What forces and peoples struggled for power?

There was a power struggle in Europe in the first half of the 1800s. Three forces were involved. **Conservatives** wanted to continue to support the kings who had ruled these lands for many centuries. These were nobles and other people who owned large amounts of property. **Liberals** wanted to give more power to elected legislatures. They were

typically middle-class merchants and business people. **Radicals** wanted the end of rule by kings and full voting rights for all. A part of these radicals did not think government was needed at all. They believed in **anarchism.**

At the same time, another movement arose in Europe—**nationalism.** This was the belief that a person's loyalty should go not to the country's ruler but to the nation itself. When the nation also had its own independent government, it became a **nation-state.** Nationalists

Lesson 2, *continued*

thought that people with a common language and culture were a nation. And they had the right to their own government. These ideas grew out of the French Revolution.

1. What goals did liberals have?

_____

_____

NATIONALISTS CHALLENGE CONSERVATIVE POWER
What changes were occurring in western Europe?

The first people to win self-rule during this period were the Greeks. Greece had been part of the Ottoman Empire for centuries. The Ottomans controlled most of the **Balkans.** That region includes most of modern Greece, Albania, Bulgaria, Romania, Turkey, and the former Yugoslavia. In 1821, the Greeks revolted against Turkish rule. They won their independence by 1830.

Other revolts broke out in Europe. In 1830, the Belgians declared their independence from rule by the Dutch. Nationalists began a long struggle to unify Italy. The Poles revolted against Russian rule. However, conservatives stopped these rebellions. New ones broke out again in 1848 among Austrian and Czech liberals. Once again, the revolts were put down forcibly.

2. How did the Greeks gain their independence?

_____

_____

RADICALS CHANGE FRANCE
Why did French radicals lose?

Events differed in France. Riots in 1830 forced the king to flee, and a new king was put in his place. Another revolt broke out in 1848. The king was overthrown and a republic established. However, the radicals who had won began arguing. Some wanted only political changes. Others wanted social and economic changes that would help the poor.

When these groups began to fight in the streets, the French gave up on the radical program. They introduced a new government. It had a legislature and a strong president. The new president was **Louis-Napoleon,** Napoleon Bonaparte's nephew. He later named himself emperor of France. He built railroads and helped industry. The economy got better, and more people had jobs.

3. What did Louis-Napoleon do for France?

_____

_____

REFORM IN RUSSIA
How did Alexander II change Russia?

In the early 1800s, Russia still did not have an industrial economy. Peasants were bound to the nobles whose land they worked.

A new ruler of Russia, **Alexander II,** decided to free the serfs. Nobles kept half their land and were paid for the other half that went to the peasants. The former serfs were not given the land. They had to pay the government for it. This debt kept them tied to the land. The czar's efforts to make changes ended when he was assassinated in 1881. Alexander III, the new czar, brought back tight control over the country.

4. How were the serfs made "free"?

_____

_____

Guided Reading Workbook

Name _____ Class _____ Date _____

Lesson 2, *continued*

As you read about uprisings in Europe, make notes in the chart to explain the outcomes of each action listed.

1. French citizens' armies win their revolution for liberty and equality. →	
2. Greeks revolt against the Ottoman Turks. →	
3. Nationalist groups in Budapest, Prague, and Vienna demand independence and self-government. →	
4. Charles X tries to set up an absolute monarchy in France. →	
5. Paris mobs overthrow monarchy of Louis-Philippe. →	
6. Louis-Napoleon Bonaparte is elected president of France and later assumes the title of Emperor Napoleon III. →	
7. In the Crimean War, Czar Nicholas I threatens to take over part of the Ottoman Empire. →	
8. Alexander II issues the Edict of Emancipation. →	

Guided Reading Workbook

Revolutions Sweep the West

Nationalism

Key Terms and People

Russification policy of forcing Russian culture on ethnic groups in the Russian Empire

Camillo di Cavour prime minister who unified northern Italy

Giuseppe Garibaldi leader of the Red Shirts who won control over parts of southern Italy

Junker wealthy German landholders

Otto von Bismarck leader who worked to expand Prussia

realpolitik tough, practical politics

kaiser emperor

Before You Read

In the last lesson, you read about revolutions and reforms in western Europe.

In this lesson, you will learn about nationalism.

As You Read

Use a timeline to list major events in the unification of Italy and Germany.

NATIONALISM: A FORCE FOR UNITY OR DISUNITY
What is nationalism?

Nationalists thought that many factors linked people to one another. First was nationality, or a common ethnic ancestry. Shared language, culture, history, and religion were also seen as ties that connected people. People sharing these traits were thought to have the right to a land they could call their own. Groups with their own government were called nation-states.

Leaders began to see that this feeling could be a powerful force for uniting a people. The French Revolution was a prime example. However, nationalism could also be a force to rip apart empires. This happened in three empires in Europe.

1. What unites people and creates a strong national feeling?

_____

_____

NATIONALISM SHAKES AGING EMPIRES
Why did nationalism divide empires?

Feelings of nationalism threatened to break apart three aging empires. The Austrian Empire was forced to split in two. One part was Austria, the other was Hungary. In Russia, harsh rule and a policy called **Russification** that forced other peoples to adopt Russian ways helped produce a revolution in 1917. This revolution overthrew the czar. Like the other two empires, the Ottoman Empire broke apart around the time of World War I.

2. Which three empires were torn apart by nationalism?

_____

_____

_____

CAVOUR UNITES ITALY
How did nationalism unite Italy?

Italians used national feeling to build a nation, not destroy an empire. Large parts of Italy were ruled by the kings of Austria and Spain. Nationalists tried to unite the nation in 1848. But the revolt was beaten down. Hopes rested with the Italian king of the state of Piedmont-Sardinia. His chief minister was Count **Camillo di Cavour.** Cavour worked to expand the king's control over other areas of the north.

Meanwhile, **Giuseppe Garibaldi** led an army of patriots that won control of southern areas. Garibaldi put the areas he conquered under control of the Italian king. In 1866, the area around Venice was added to the king's control. By 1870, the king completed the uniting of Italy.

3. Who helped unify Italy?

_____

_____

_____

BISMARCK UNITES GERMANY; A SHIFT IN POWER
How was Germany united?

Germany had also been divided into many different states for many centuries. In 1815, the states formed a league, called the German Confederation. Prussia and Austria-Hungary controlled this group. Over time, Prussia rose to become more powerful with the support of wealthy landowners called **Junkers.** Leading this move was prime minister **Otto von Bismarck.** Bismarck was a master of **realpolitik**—tough power politics.

Bismarck worked to create a new confederation of German states. Prussia controlled it. To win the loyalty of German areas in the south, he purposefully angered a weak France so that it would declare war on Prussia. Prussia won the Franco-Prussian War in 1871. The war with France gave the southern German states a nationalistic feeling. They joined the other states in naming the king of Prussia as emperor, or **kaiser,** of a strong united Germany.

These events changed the balance of power in Europe. Germany and Britain were the strongest powers, followed by France. Austria, Russia, and Italy were all even weaker.

4. What was the result of the defeat of France and the uniting of Germany?

_____

_____

Lesson 3, *continued*

As you read this lesson, fill in the timeline to review the events that took place in Italy and Germany.

1848	Italy		1.
	Germany	→	2.
1852	Italy	→	3.
1856	Germany	→	4.
1860	Italy	→	5.
1862	Germany	→	6.
1866	Germany	→	7.
1870	Italy	→	8.
1871	Germany	→	9.

Guided Reading Workbook

Revolutions in the Arts

Key Terms and People

romanticism movement in art and ideas that focused on nature and the thoughts and feelings of individuals

realism movement in art that tried to show life as it really was

deism belief that everyone is born with religious, ethical, and moral impulses

impressionism style of art using light and light-filled colors to produce an "impression"

Before You Read

In the last lesson, you read how political borders changed in Europe.

In this lesson, you will learn about changes in the arts in Europe.

As You Read

Use a chart to note details about movements in the arts.

THE ROMANTIC MOVEMENT
What is romanticism?

In the early 1800s, the Enlightenment gradually gave way to another movement, called **romanticism.** This movement in art and ideas focused on nature and on the thoughts and feelings of individuals. Gone was the idea that reason and order were good things. Romantic thinkers valued feeling, not reason, and nature, not society. Romantic thinkers held idealized views of the past as simpler, better times. They valued the common people. As a result, they enjoyed folk stories, songs, and traditions. They also supported calls for democracy. However, not all romantic artists and thinkers supported all of these ideas.

Romantic writers had different themes. During the first half of the 19th century, the Grimm brothers collected German folk tales. They also created a German dictionary and worked on German grammar. These works celebrated being German long before there was a united German nation. Other writers wrote about strong individuals. Some wrote about beauty and nature.

Germany produced one of the greatest early Romantic writers. Johann Wolfgang von Goethe wrote *The Sorrows of Young Werther*. It was a story about a young man who kills himself after he falls in love with a married woman.

Lesson 4, *continued*

British Romantic poets William Wordsworth and Samuel Taylor Coleridge honored nature as the source of truth and beauty. A type of horror story called a Gothic novel became popular. Novels such as Mary Shelley's *Frankenstein* were tales about good and evil.

Romanticism was important in music as well. Composers wrote music to appeal to the hearts and souls of listeners. Ludwig van Beethoven, a German, was the foremost of these composers. Romanticism made music a popular art form.

1. What did Romantic thinkers and artists value?

   _____

   _____

THE SHIFT TO REALISM IN THE ARTS
What is realism?

In the middle 1800s, the grim realities of industrial life made the dreams of romanticism seem silly. A new movement arose—**realism.** Artists and writers tried to show life as it really was. They used their art to protest unfair social conditions. French writer Emile Zola's books revealed harsh working conditions for the poor. They led to new laws aimed at helping those people. In England, Charles Dickens wrote many novels that showed how poor people suffered in the new industrial economy.

A new device, the camera, was developed in this period. Photographers used cameras to capture realistic images on film.

2. For what purposes did writers use realism?

   _____

   _____

IMPRESSIONISTS REACT AGAINST REALISM
What is impressionism?

In the 1860s, Parisian painters reacted against the realistic style. This new art style—**impressionism**—used light and light-filled colors to produce an impression of a subject or moment in time. The style focused on the positive, showing people enjoying life. Impressionist artists like Claude Monet and Pierre-Auguste Renoir glorified the delights of the life of the rising middle class in their paintings. Composers created music that set a mood by using different musical structures, instruments, or patterns.

3. What was the focus of Impressionist art and music?

   _____

   _____

Lesson 4, *continued*

As you read this lesson, take notes to answer questions about the
artistic and intellectual movements of the 1800s.

Nationalism ushers in a romantic movement in arts and ideas.	
1. How did the Ideas of romanticism contrast with Enlightenment ideas?	2. How were the ideas of romanticism reflected in literature?
3. How was romanticism reflected in art?	4. How did romanticism affect the music of the time?
Realism in art and literature replaces Romantic idealism.	
5. What trends or events led to a shift from romanticism to realism?	6. How did photography exemplify the art of the new industrial age?
7. What were some themes common to realist novels?	8. What did realist novelists accomplish with their exposés?

Guided Reading Workbook

The Beginnings of Industrialization

Key Terms and People

Industrial Revolution great increase in machine production that began in England in the 18th century

enclosure large closed-in field for farming

crop rotation planting a different crop in the same field each year to allow the soil to regenerate

industrialization process of developing machine production of goods

factors of production conditions needed to produce goods and services

factory building where goods are made

entrepreneur person who organizes, manages, and takes on the financial risk of a business enterprise

Henry Bessemer British engineer who developed a way to mass-produce steel cheaply

Before You Read

In the last lesson, you read about romanticism and realism in the arts.

In this lesson, you will read about the beginning of the Industrial Revolution.

As You Read

Answer questions in a chart to note important events in Britain's industrialization.

INDUSTRIAL REVOLUTION BEGINS IN BRITAIN
How did the Industrial Revolution begin?

The **Industrial Revolution** was the great increase in production that began in England during the 18th century. Before the Industrial Revolution, people made most goods by hand. By the middle of the 1700s, more and more goods were made by machines.

The Industrial Revolution began with an agricultural revolution. In the early 1700s, large landowners in Britain bought much of the land that had been owned by poorer farmers. The landowners collected these lands into large fields closed in by fences or hedges. These fields were called **enclosures.** Many of the poor farmers who lost their lands became tenant farmers. Others gave up farming and moved to the cities. The growth in the number of people in cities to work in factories helped create the Industrial Revolution.

New farm methods made farmers more productive. For example, Jethro Tull invented a seed drill that made planting more efficient. Farmers also practiced **crop rotation.** Crop rotation is the practice of planting a different crop in the same field each year. This improves the quality of the soil.

Industrialization is the process of developing machine production of goods. For several reasons, Britain was the first country to industrialize.

Great Britain had all the resources needed for industrialization. These resources included coal, water, iron ore, rivers, harbors, and banks. Britain also had all the **factors of production** that the Industrial Revolution required. These factors of production included land, labor (workers), and capital (wealth).

1. Why was Britain the first country to industrialize?

_____

_____

INVENTIONS SPUR INDUSTRIALIZATION
What inventions helped change business?

The Industrial Revolution began in the textile industry. Several new inventions helped businesses make cloth and clothing more quickly. Richard Arkwright invented the water frame in 1769. It used water power to run spinning machines that made yarn. In 1779, Samuel Compton invented the spinning mule, which made better thread. In 1787, Edmund Cartwright developed the power loom. The power loom was a machine that sped up the cloth-making process.

These new inventions were large and expensive machines. They needed large **factories** to house and run these machines. **Entrepreneurs,** or people who start and manage businesses, built the factories near rivers because these machines ran on water power.

2. How was the textile industry changed by the new inventions?

_____

_____

IMPROVEMENTS IN TRANSPORTATION; THE RAILWAY AGE BEGINS

The invention of the steam engine in 1705 brought in a new source of power. The steam engine used fire to heat water and produce steam. The power of the steam drove the engine. Eventually steam-driven engines were used to run factories and shipping boats.

Starting in the 1820s, steam brought a new burst of industrial growth. George Stephenson, a British engineer, set up the world's first railroad line. It used a steam-driven locomotive. **Henry Bessemer,** a British engineer, devised a way to make steel in large quantities. Railroad rails were made using the inexpensive steel. Soon, railroads were being built all over Britain.

The railroad boom helped business owners move their goods to market more quickly. These changes created thousands of new jobs in several different industries. Millions of British people, including the middle class, also enjoyed the trains. Even Queen Victoria regularly traveled by train.

3. What effects did the invention of the steam engine have?

_____

_____

As you read this lesson, make notes in the chart to explain how each
factor listed contributed to an Industrial Revolution in Great Britain.

1. Agricultural revolution	
2. Abundant natural resources	
3. Political stability	
4. Factors of production	
5. Technological advances in the textile industry	
6. Entrepreneurs	
7. Building of factories	
8. Railroad boom	

The Industrial Revolution

Lesson 2

Industrialization

Key Terms and People

urbanization city building and the movement of people to cities

middle class social class of skilled workers, professionals, business people, and wealthy farmers

Before You Read

In the last lesson, you read about the Industrial Revolution.

In this lesson, you will read about some of its effects.

As You Read

Use an outline to organize the summaries' main ideas and details.

INDUSTRIALIZATION CHANGES LIFE

How did industrialization change people's ways of life?

Industrialization brought many changes to the British people. More people could use coal to heat their homes, eat better food, and wear better clothing.

Another change was **urbanization**— city building and the movement of people to cities. For centuries, most people in Europe had lived in the country. By the 1800s, more and more people lived in cities, where they had come to find jobs.

Living conditions were bad in crowded cities. Many people could not find good housing, schools, or police protection. Filth, garbage, and sickness were part of life in the slums. A person in a city could expect to live 17 years. In

the countryside, a person could expect to live 38 years.

Working conditions were also bad. The average worker spent 14 hours a day on the job, 6 days a week. Many workers were killed or seriously injured in accidents.

1. What were major changes in living conditions and working conditions?

_____

_____

CLASS TENSIONS GROW; POSITIVE EFFECTS OF THE INDUSTRIAL REVOLUTION

Who were the members of the middle class?

Some people's lives were improved in the new economy. The Industrial Revolution created new wealth for the

middle class, which included skilled workers, professionals, business people, and wealthy farmers. People in the middle class enjoyed comfortable lives in pleasant homes. This class began to grow in size. Some people grew wealthier than the nobles who had been in control for many centuries.

The Industrial Revolution had many good effects. It created wealth. It created jobs for workers and over time helped many of them live better lives. It produced better diets, better housing, and better clothing at lower prices.

2. How did industrialization affect the middle class?

_____

_____

THE MILLS OF MANCHESTER
***What* changes occurred in Manchester?**

The English city of Manchester is a good example of how industrialization changed society. Rapid growth made the city crowded and filthy. The factory owners risked their money and worked long hours to make their businesses grow. In return, they enjoyed huge profits and built huge houses. The workers also worked long hours but had few benefits. Many of these workers were children, some only six years old. The British government did not limit the use of children as workers until 1819.

The large amount of industry in Manchester caused environmental problems. Coal smoke and cloth dyes from the factories polluted the air and water. Yet Manchester also created many jobs, a variety of consumer goods, and great wealth.

3. Why is Manchester a good example of how industrialization changed cities?

_____

_____

Lesson 2, *continued*

As you read this case study, answer the questions to consider how industrialization changed the way people lived and worked.

What changes did industrialization bring about for the following groups of people?	
1. Poor city dwellers	
2. Factory workers	
3. Wealthy merchants, factory owners, shippers	
4. Children	
5. Lower middle class of factory overseers and skilled workers	
6. Large landowners and aristocrats	

What were the long-term consequences of the Industrial Revolution for each of the following?	
7. The environment	8. Education

The Industrial Revolution

Industrialization Spreads

Key Terms and People

mass production system of manufacturing large quantities of identical items

interchangeable parts machine parts that are identical and manufactured by machine

assembly line each worker does one step of a manufacturing processes

division of labor different workers doing individual and different tasks

specialization separation of tasks

economic interdependence people in a society relying on other people

stock right of ownership in a company called a corporation

corporation business owned by stockholders who share in its profits but are not responsible for its debts

Before You Read

In the last lesson, you read about some of the effects of industrialization.

In this lesson, you will see how industrialization spread to other nations.

As You Read

Use a chart to compare industrialization in the United States, in Europe, and around the world.

INDUSTRIAL DEVELOPMENT IN THE UNITED STATES
How did industrialization begin in the United States?

The United States was one of the first to industrialize after Great Britain. Like Britain, the United States had a great deal of coal and water to create power. There was also plenty of iron. In addition, immigrants in the United States created a large supply of workers.

The United States also benefited from conflict with Britain. During the War of 1812, Britain stopped shipping goods to the United States. As a result, American industries began to make many of the goods that Americans wanted.

In the United States, industrialization began in the textile industry. In 1789, Samuel Slater, a British worker, brought the secret of Britain's textile machines to North America. Slater built a machine to spin thread.

In 1813, a group of Massachusetts investors built textile factories in Waltham, Massachusetts. Just a few years later they built even more factories in the Massachusetts town of Lowell.

Guided Reading Workbook

Thousands of workers, mostly young girls, came to work in the factories.

Americans developed the system of making a large amount of the same product, called **mass production.** Machines use identical parts, called **interchangeable parts.** These parts can be mass produced quickly and then assembled so that the machines work exactly the same. Replacement parts are easy to get, and they fit perfectly.

Changes were made in factories, too. Products moved from worker to worker on an **assembly line.** Each worker did one step of the work. Having different workers do different tasks is called **division of labor.** Workers learn a specific task. Separating tasks to make a process more efficient is called **specialization.**

Industrialization caused **economic interdependence.** People needed the resources of other people. People did not have to make everything they needed.

Businesses needed huge sums of money to do big projects. To raise money, companies sold **stock.** Stocks are shares of ownership in a company. All those who held stock were part owners of the company. This form of business organization is called a **corporation.**

1. How did industrialization begin in the United States?

   _____

   _____

CONTINENTAL EUROPE INDUSTRIALIZES
Where did industrialization begin in continental Europe?

Industrial growth also spread from England to the European continent. Belgium was the first to industrialize.

It was rich in iron and coal. The country also had good waterways.

Germany was divided politically until the late 1800s. However, the Ruhr Valley in western Germany was rich in coal. It became a leading industrial region.

Industrial growth did not occur in France until after 1830. It was helped by the government's construction of a large network of railroads. Austria-Hungary and Spain faced transportation problems that held them back from industrializing.

2. Which nation industrialized first, and why?

   _____

   _____

THE IMPACT OF INDUSTRIALIZATION
How did industrialization change the world?

The countries of Europe soon began to take advantage of Africa and Asia. Europeans wanted to use these lands as sources of raw materials for their factories.

The European nations took control of lands in many areas of the world outside of Europe. This practice is called imperialism.

The Industrial Revolution that took place in the 1700s and 1800s changed life forever in the countries that industrialized. Problems caused by industrialization led to movements for social reform.

3. How did industrialization lead to imperialism?

   _____

   _____

Name _____ Class _____ Date _____

Lesson 3, *continued*

As you read this lesson, take notes to answer the questions about industrialization in different parts of the world.

Industrial development in the United States paralleled industrialization in Britain.	
1. What were some favorable conditions that sparked industrialization in both Britain and the United States?	
2. What factors led to the great expansion of U.S. industry in the late 1800s?	
Industrialization eventually reached continental Europe.	
3. How did the Napoleonic wars affect the development of industry in Europe?	
4. How would you characterize the expansion of industry throughout Europe during the early 1800s?	
Industrialization revolutionized every aspect of society worldwide.	
5. How did industrialization shift the world balance of power?	
6. In what ways did industrialization benefit society?	

The Industrial Revolution

Reforming the Industrial World

Key Terms and People

laissez faire economic theory that argues that governments should not interfere with business affairs

Adam Smith philosopher who defended laissez-faire economics

capitalism economic system in which people invest money to make a profit

utilitarianism belief that an idea is only as good as it is useful

socialism belief that businesses should be owned by society as a whole

Karl Marx economic thinker who wrote about a radical form of socialism

communism form of socialism in which all production is owned by the people

anarchism belief that people should be able to develop freely without government interferance

union organized groups of workers that bargain with business owners to get better pay and working conditions

strike organized refusal to work

Before You Read

In the last lesson, you read about how industrialization spread to different nations.

In this lesson, you will learn about new ideas and reforms.

As You Read

Use a chart to summarize the characteristics of capitalism and socialism.

THE PHILOSOPHERS OF INDUSTRIALIZATION
What is capitalism?

Industrialization led to new ways of thinking about society. Some economists thought that the government should leave business owners alone. This view is called **laissez faire.**

Adam Smith argued that governments should not put limits on business. He and others, including British economists Thomas Malthus and David Ricardo, supported a system called **capitalism.** In a capitalist economy, people invest their money in businesses to make a profit.

Smith and the others believed that society would benefit over time from this system. Supporters of laissez faire opposed laws to protect workers.

1. How does capitalism work?

_____

_____

THE RISE OF SOCIALISM; MARXISM: RADICAL SOCIALISM
What is socialism?

Other thinkers challenged capitalism. One group was called the **utilitarians.** They thought it was unfair that workers should work so hard for such little pay and live in such poor conditions.

Some thinkers wanted society as a whole to own businesses. This way, all people would enjoy the benefits of increased production. This view—called **socialism**—grew out of a belief in progress and a concern for justice.

A German thinker named **Karl Marx** proposed a form of socialism that became known as Marxism. He said that factory owners and workers would struggle for power. Over time, he said, the capitalist system would destroy itself.

Marx wrote *The Communist Manifesto.* It described **communism,** a form of socialism in which production is controlled by the people.

Anarchism also gained popularity during this time. Anarchists believe government is harmful. Some believers went too far. Between 1890 and 1901, a number of politicians were killed and terrorist acts were carried out.

2. How are the ideas of capitalism and socialism different?

_____

_____

LABOR UNIONS AND REFORM LAWS
How did workers take action to improve their lives?

While thinkers discussed these ideas, workers fought to improve their lives. Many workers joined **unions.** A union is a group of workers that tries to bargain with employers for better pay and better working conditions.

When employers resisted these efforts, the workers went on **strike,** or refused to work. British and American workers struggled for a long time for the right to form unions.

Britain also passed laws to limit how much work women and children could do. Groups in the United States pushed for similar laws.

3. How did both the government and workers themselves try to improve workers' lives?

_____

_____

THE REFORM MOVEMENT SPREADS
What other reforms were taking place at this time?

Ending slavery was a major reform movement of the 1800s. The British Parliament ended the slave trade in 1807. It then abolished slavery in British territories in 1833.

Slavery was finally abolished in the United States in 1865, after the Civil War. Spain ended slavery in Puerto Rico in 1873 and in Cuba in 1886. Brazil was the last country to ban slavery, in 1888.

Women were active in many reform movements. Many women fought for equal rights for women. In 1888, women from around the world formed a group dedicated to this cause.

Reformers took on other projects as well. They pushed to improve education and the conditions in prisons.

4. Name two major reform movements of the 1800s.

_____

_____

Guided Reading Workbook

As you read about the age of reforms, take notes to answer the
questions about the ideas of the philosophers and reformers of the
Industrial Revolution.

The Economic Philosophers	What were the basic ideas of each philosopher?
1. Adam Smith	
2. Thomas Malthus	
3. David Ricardo	

The Social Reformers	How did each reformer try to correct the ills of industrialization?
4. John Stuart Mill	
5. Robert Owen	
6. Charles Fourier and Henri de Saint-Simon	
7. Karl Marx and Friedrich Engels	
8. William Wilberforce	
9. Jane Addams	
10. Horace Mann	

An Age of Democracy and Progress

Democratic Reform and Activism

Key Terms and People

suffrage right to vote

Chartist movement movement in England to give the right to vote to more people and to obtain other rights

Queen Victoria leader of Britain when democratic changes were occurring

Third Republic government formed in France after Napoleon III was exiled

Dreyfus affair events surrounding the framing of a Jewish officer in the French army

anti-Semitism prejudice against Jews

Zionism movement to establish a separate homeland in Palestine for the Jews

Before You Read

In the last lesson, you read about the Industrial Revolution.

In this lesson, you will read about democratic reforms in Great Britain and France.

As You Read

Use a timeline to answer questions about democratic reform in Great Britain.

BRITAIN ENACTS REFORMS
How did Britain become more democratic?

Since the 1600s, Britain's government had been a constitutional monarchy. A king or queen ruled the country, but the elected legislature—Parliament—held the real power.

Still, very few people could vote for members of Parliament. Only men who owned property—about 5 percent of the population—had the right to vote. This changed in the 1800s. The Reform Bill of 1832 was the first step. Middle-class people across England protested the fact that they could not vote. Worried by revolutions sweeping Europe, Parliament passed the Reform Bill. This law gave **suffrage,** the right to vote, to many in the middle class.

Those who still could not vote began the **Chartist Movement.** They wanted the vote and other rights. They presented their demands to Parliament in the People's Charter of 1838. Although they did not get what they wanted at first, over time their demands became law.

The leader of England during all these changes was **Queen Victoria.** She was queen for nearly 64 years. She performed her duties wisely and capably, but Parliament gained more power.

The era when she was queen is known as the Victorian Age.

1. How did power shift in Britain in the 1800s?

_____

_____

WOMEN GET THE VOTE
How did women campaign for the right to vote?

By 1890, a few countries had given the right to vote to all men. But none gave the right to vote to all women. In the 1800s, women in the United States and Britain campaigned peacefully for the vote.

In 1903, a group called the Women's Social and Political Union began a stronger campaign for women's suffrage in Britain. This campaign included rallies, parades, and demonstrations during speeches of government officials. But women in Britain and the United States did not win the right to vote until after World War I.

2. When did women get the right to vote in Britain and the United States?

_____

_____

FRANCE AND DEMOCRACY
What was the Dreyfus affair?

The road to democracy in France was rocky. France lost a war with Prussia. The National Assembly met to decide

on a new government. Finally, in 1875, a new government—the **Third Republic**—was formed. It lasted over 60 years. They were years marked by fighting between many political parties.

In the 1890s, French society was divided over the case of an army officer named Alfred Dreyfus. Dreyfus was accused of being a traitor. The charge was made mainly because Dreyfus was a Jew. Many people believed the charge was true. Dreyfus was found guilty. The issue became known as the **Dreyfus affair.** A few years later, evidence showed that Dreyfus had been framed. He was later declared innocent.

The Dreyfus affair revealed **anti-Semitism,** or prejudice against Jews, in Europe. In eastern Europe, anti-Semitism was bad. The Russian government even allowed organized attacks on Jewish villages. From the 1880s on, many Jews fled to the United States. In the 1890s, a movement called **Zionism** began. Its goal was a separate homeland for the Jews in Palestine.

3. Where in Europe was anti-Semitism found?

_____

_____

As you read about democratic reforms in Great Britain, answer the
questions about the timeline.

1830	**Revolution breaks out in France.**	1. How did this revolution affect parliamentary leaders in Britain?
1832	**Parliament passes the Reform Bill.**	
1837	**Queen Victoria comes to the throne.**	2. How did this bill advance democracy in Great Britain?
1838	**Chartists submit the People's Charter to Parliament.**	
		3. Why did the British monarchy become so powerless in the 1800s?
1867	**Parliament extends suffrage to working-class men.**	4. What demands did the Chartists make in their petition?
1884	**Parliament extends suffrage to male rural workers.**	5. Why did ordinary people went a greater voice in government?
		6. What were the objectives of this group?
1903	**Emmeline Pankhurst forms the Women's Social and Political Union.**	

Guided Reading Workbook

An Age of Democracy and Progress

Lesson 2

Self-Rule for British Colonies

Key Terms and People

dominion nation in the British Empire allowed to govern its own domestic affairs

Maori Polynesian people who settled in New Zealand

Aborigines native people of Australia

penal colony place where convicts are sent to serve their sentences as an alternative to prison

home rule local control over domestic affairs

Irish Republican Army unofficial military force seeking independence

Before You Read

In the last lesson, you read about democracy and prejudice in Britain, France, and other parts of Europe.

In this lesson, you will read about the fight for self-rule in British colonies.

As You Read

Use a chart to note causes and effects of significant events in Canada, Australia, New Zealand, and Ireland.

CANADA STRUGGLES FOR SELF-RULE
How was the dominion of Canada formed?

Britain had colonies all over the world. Three of them—Canada, Australia, and New Zealand—were settled by colonists from Europe. Over time, the people in these colonies wanted to control their own governments.

The white settlers of Canada were split into two groups. One group included French-speaking Catholics who lived in the colony. Britain had won Canada from France in 1763. The other group was English-speaking and mostly Protestant. The two groups did not get

along. In 1791, Britain split the colony into two provinces. Each colony had its own government.

But the French-speaking people were not happy with British rule. After several rebellions, the British Parliament put the two provinces back together under one government. Other smaller colonies were added to create the Dominion of Canada. As a **dominion,** Canada had the right to make all laws concerning its own affairs. But Parliament kept the right to control Canadian relations with other countries. By 1871, Canada stretched all the way from the Atlantic Ocean to the Pacific Ocean.

Guided Reading Workbook

1. Why does Canada today contain both French-speaking and English-speaking people?

_____

_____

AUSTRALIA AND NEW ZEALAND
How were Australia and New Zealand settled?

New Zealand became part of the British Empire in 1769. Britain claimed Australia in 1770. Both lands were already inhabited: the **Maori** lived in New Zealand and the **Aborigines** lived in Australia. The Aborigines, as Europeans later called the native people of Australia, were nomadic. They fished and hunted.

Australia was a **penal colony.** The first British settlers there were convicted criminals. The settlement of New Zealand went slowly because the British government recognized that the native people—the Maori—had rights to the land. In contrast, the Aborigines in Australia had almost no rights. By the 1840s, though, the number of British settlers in New Zealand was growing.

During the 1850s, Australia and New Zealand became self-governing. But they stayed in the British Empire. In the early 1900s they became dominions. Australia was the first country to use the secret ballot in elections. New Zealand—in 1893—was the first country to give women the right to vote.

2. How were the native people of Australia and New Zealand treated differently?

_____

_____

THE IRISH WIN HOME RULE
Why did the British hesitate to give Ireland independence?

Irish self-rule took a long time to achieve. The Irish opposed English rule from its start in the 1100s. Religious conflict also divided the Catholic Irish and the small group of Irish Protestants who lived in the north.

In the 1840s, the Irish suffered a terrible famine. Many died of starvation and disease. Others lost their land. Millions of Irish people emigrated, or left Ireland. Most went to the United States or Britain.

In the late 1800s, some Irish pushed for complete independence. Most argued for **home rule**—the right to govern internal affairs. The British government opposed this move. They were afraid that the Catholic majority would treat the Protestants in the north harshly. In 1914, Parliament enacted a home rule bill for the southern part of Ireland. When World War I delayed its enactment, Irish nationalists rebelled. The **Irish Republican Army,** a military force seeking independence, attacked British officials in Ireland.

Finally, Britain split Ireland in two. Northern Ireland remained part of Britain. The southern part became independent. Violence continued in Ireland off and on for decades.

3. What was one reason why Ireland was split into two parts?

_____

_____

As you read this lesson, note some of the causes and effects of conflicts between Britain and its colonies.

Causes	Actions/Events	Effects
	1. Parliament creates Upper Canada and Lower Canada in 1791.	
	2. Nova Scotia and New Brunswick join with the Province of Canada to form the Dominion of Canada in 1867.	
	3. British annex New Zealand in 1838.	
	4. British government formally joins Ireland to Britain in 1801.	
	5. During the Great Famine, the British government forces Irish peasants to continue paying rent.	
	6. Irish nationalists rebel in Dublin in 1916.	

An Age of Democracy and Progress

War and Expansion in the United States

Key Terms and People

manifest destiny belief that the United States would rule the land from the Atlantic Ocean to the Pacific Ocean

Abraham Lincoln 16th president of the United States

secede to leave a nation

U.S. Civil War war fought between the North and South from 1861 to 1865

Emancipation Proclamation 1863 proclamation to free the slaves in the Confederate states

segregation separation by race

Before You Read

In the last lesson, you read about the struggle for self-rule in British colonies.

In this lesson, you will read about changes in the United States during the same time period.

As You Read

Take notes on major events in the United States in the 19th century.

AMERICANS MOVE WEST
What was manifest destiny?

The United States expanded across North America and fought a bloody civil war. In the early 1800s the nation grew in size. It bought a huge piece of land from France in the Louisiana Purchase. It gained Florida and part of the Oregon Territory. Soon it stretched from the Atlantic to the Pacific oceans.

Many believed in **manifest destiny**—the belief that the United States would control land from the Atlantic Ocean to the Pacific. As white settlers moved farther west, Native Americans suffered. In the 1830s, thousands of Native Americans were forced to move from their homes in the east to the present state of Oklahoma.

The Native Americans were forced to go to new land that was not very good. The government continued to push them off their original land.

1. What problems did the movement westward bring?

_____

_____

CIVIL WAR TESTS DEMOCRACY
Why was the Civil War fought?

The growth of the nation raised serious questions. The southern states used slave labor to grow crops such as cotton. People in the South hoped to extend slavery to the western lands. But many northerners believed that slavery was wrong and should be ended.

Abraham Lincoln was elected president in 1860. The southerners did not like him at all because he promised to stop slavery.

The southern states **seceded,** or pulled out of, the Union. The southerners formed their own nation known as the Confederate States of America. The struggle over slavery led to the **U.S. Civil War.** War broke out after Confederate forces fired on a Union fort in 1861. The fighting lasted four years.

The North won the war. During the war, President Abraham Lincoln issued the **Emancipation Proclamation.** This proclamation declared that the people enslaved in the Confederate states were free. After the war, the Constitution was amended, or changed, to outlaw slavery. Another change to the Constitution made African Americans citizens.

In the first few years after the war, newly freed African Americans enjoyed equal rights. But whites soon regained control of the governments of the southern states. They passed laws that took away the rights of blacks. The white governments also set up **segregation,** or separation, of blacks and whites. African Americans have continued to fight for equality since then.

2. What changes came about as a result of the Civil War?

_____

_____

THE POSTWAR ECONOMY
What happened after the war?

After the Civil War, the nation experienced quick industrial growth. A sharp rise in immigration from Europe and Asia helped cause this growth. By 1914, more than 20 million people had come to the United States.

These new citizens moved to cities in the northeast and midwest. Many moved to the open spaces of the west.

In addition, Congress set aside money to build a railroad across the continent. The railroad linked the different regions of the nation. By 1900, nearly 200,000 miles of track crossed the country. The growth of the railroads helped American industry grow.

3. What helped cause the rise in industrial growth?

_____

_____

Lesson 3, *continued*

As you read this lesson, take notes to answer the questions about the
United States in the 19th century.

From 1783 to 1853, the United States adds new territory	
1. What was the significance of the Louisiana Purchase?	
2. How did the United States extend its northern and southern boundaries?	
3. What lands did the United States acquire as a result of the Mexican–American War?	
4. How did the idea of manifest destiny affect Native Americans?	
Civil War breaks out between the North and South	
5. What issues caused conflict between the North and South?	
6. What were the immediate causes of the U.S. Civil War?	
7. Why did Abraham Lincoln issue the Emancipation Proclamation?	
8. What were the long-term economic effects of the Civil War?	

An Age of Democracy and Progress

Nineteenth-Century Progress

Key Terms and People

telegraph a machine that sent messages instantly over wires

assembly line arrangement by which a product in a factory is moved from worker to worker, with each worker completing a single step in the task

Charles Darwin scientist who developed the theory of evolution

theory of evolution theory that all life on earth developed from simpler forms of life

radioactivity form of energy released as atoms decay

psychology study of the mind

mass culture art and entertainment appealing to a large audience

Before You Read

In the last lesson, you read about political change in the United States.

In this lesson, you will learn about progress in science and other fields.

As You Read

Answer questions about things famous inventors and scientists innovated and developed.

INVENTIONS MAKE LIFE EASIER
How did inventions change ways of life?

In the late 1800s, new inventions changed how people lived. Inventors around the world worked to make new machines. Thomas Edison received patents on more than 1,000 inventions. Among them were the electric light bulb and the phonograph.

Samuel Morse invented the **telegraph** in 1837. This was an important first step in communication. Shortly after, Alexander Graham Bell invented the telephone. Then Guglielmo Marconi created the first radio.

There were changes in transportation, too. Henry Ford made the car affordable to ordinary people. He had a factory with an **assembly line.** It allowed him to build cheap cars. These cars were affordable for ordinary people. In 1903, the Wright brothers flew the first motor-powered airplane flight. Soon there was an aircraft industry.

1. What were three important inventions during this period?

_____

_____

NEW IDEAS IN MEDICINE
What new ideas appeared in medicine?

Until the mid-1800s, no one knew about germs. French scientist Louis Pasteur discovered that microscopic animals could live in food. Pasteur called these tiny creatures bacteria. Scientists soon realized that bacteria could cause disease.

Doctors and health officials saw the importance of keeping public places clean. Hospitals and cities became cleaner and more modern. Fewer people got sick.

At the same time, researchers developed cures for diseases. People began to live longer, healthier lives.

2. What relevance did Pasteur's ideas have to the treatment of disease?

_____

_____

NEW IDEAS IN SCIENCE
What new ideas appeared in science?

English scientist **Charles Darwin** developed the **theory of evolution.** This theory said that all life on earth had developed from simpler life forms over millions of years. This theory was hotly debated. Many people did not accept this idea. They said it went against the Bible.

In the mid-1880s, an Austrian monk named Gregor Mendel showed that parents passed on their personal traits to their offspring. The science of genetics began.

Other scientists made new discoveries in chemistry and physics. They found that all matter is made of tiny particles called atoms. Marie and Pierre Curie discovered **radioactivity.** Radioactivity is the energy that is released when atoms decay.

3. Tell what each discovered or developed: Charles Darwin, Gregor Mendel, Marie and Pierre Curie.

_____

_____

SOCIAL SCIENCES EXPLORE BEHAVIOR
What is psychology?

In the late 1800s, some thinkers began to study the human mind. This new social science was called **psychology.** The Russian scientist Ivan Pavlov conducted a series of experiments

Sigmund Freud, an Austrian doctor, argued that a person's actions are shaped by forces in the subconscious mind. These views shocked many. They seemed to overturn the idea that people could use their reason to build better lives.

4. What did Freud reveal about the mind?

_____

_____

THE RISE OF MASS CULTURE
What is mass culture?

With the rise of the middle class, a new mass culture developed.

This new **mass culture** appealed to a wide audience. People went to music halls to enjoy singing and dancing. In the early 1900s, they watched the first silent movies. People also enjoyed sporting events, both as participants and as spectators.

5. What new forms of entertainment became popular?

_____

_____

Name _____ Class _____ Date _____

As you read this lesson, take notes to answer the questions about the technological and scientific advances of the late 1800s.

The Inventors	What were their most significant inventions or innovations?
1. Thomas Edison	
2. Alexander Graham Bell	
3. Guglielmo Marconi	
4. Henry Ford	
5. Wilbur and Orville Wright	
The Scientists	**What were their most significant discoveries or theories?**
6. Louis Pasteur	
7. Charles Darwin	
8. Gregor Mendel	
9. Marie and Pierre Curie	
10. Ivan Pavlov	

The Age of Imperialism

The Roots of Imperialism

Key Terms and People

imperialism control by a strong nation over a weaker nation

racism belief that one race is superior to others

Social Darwinism use of Charles Darwin's ideas about evolution to explain human societies

Berlin Conference meeting at which Europeans agreed on rules for colonizing Africa

Shaka Zulu chief who created a large centralized state

Boer Dutch colonist in South Africa

Boer War war between the British and the Boers

Before You Read

In the last lesson you learned about progress in science and other fields.

In this lesson, you will learn about the European colonization of Africa.

As You Read

Use a chart to list the forces and events surrounding imperialism in Africa.

AFRICA BEFORE EUROPEAN DOMINATION; FORCES DRIVING IMPERIALISM

Why did imperialism begin in the 1800s?

In the early 1800s, Europeans controlled a few areas along the coast of Africa. By the mid-1800s, Europeans were expanding their control to new lands. This policy is called **imperialism.**

There were four basic reasons for imperialism. The first reason for imperialism had to do with money. Europeans wanted colonies to provide raw materials for their factories. The

Europeans also wanted to sell their goods in their new colonies.

National pride was a second reason for imperialism. Some nations wanted to gain colonies to show their national strength.

Racism was a third reason for imperialism. Racism is the belief that one race is better than others. Many Europeans believed that whites were better than other races.

Racism is related to Social Darwinism. **Social Darwinism** is the use of Charles Darwin's ideas about evolution to explain human societies.

Guided Reading Workbook

Lesson 1, *continued*

One of Darwin's ideas was "survival of the fittest." This idea was that the fittest, or strongest, species would survive. Weak species would not survive.

People who believed in Social Darwinism argued that fit people and nations survived. They also believed that weak people and nations would not survive.

The fourth reason is that Christian missionaries also supported imperialism. They thought that European rule would end the slave trade. The missionaries also wanted to convert the people of other continents to Christianity.

Europeans began to take lands in Africa for these reasons. Technology helped the Europeans succeed. The African peoples were divided. It was hard for them to resist European advances.

1. What are four reasons for imperialism?

_____

_____

THE DIVISION OF AFRICA
How did European nations claim African lands?

The "scramble for Africa" began in the 1880s. Diamonds were discovered in South Africa in 1867. Gold was discovered there in 1886. Europeans became more interested in the continent.

The European nations did not want to fight over the land. They met at the **Berlin Conference** in 1884–1885. They agreed that any nation could claim any part of Africa by telling the others and

by showing that it had control of the area. Europeans quickly grabbed land. By 1914, only Liberia and Ethiopia were free from European control.

2. What was the purpose of the Berlin Conference?

_____

_____

THREE GROUPS CLASH OVER SOUTH AFRICA
What groups fought over South Africa?

In South Africa, three groups struggled over the land. In the early 1800s, the Zulu chief **Shaka** fought to win more land. Shaka's successors were not able to keep his kingdom intact. The Zulu land was taken over by the British in 1887.

Meanwhile, the British took control of the Dutch colony on the southern coast. Thousands of Dutch settlers, called **Boers,** moved north to escape the British. This movement is known as the Great Trek. The Boers fought the Zulus whose land they were entering.

At the end of the century, Boers fought a vicious war against the British called the **Boer War.** The Boers lost this war. The Boers then joined the British-run Union of South Africa.

3. Who were the Boers, and who did they fight?

_____

_____

Lesson 1, *continued*

As you read about the European colonization of Africa, fill out the
chart by writing notes in the appropriate spaces.

The Forces of Imperialism	
1. Note three motives behind the European race for colonies.	
2. Note two technological advantages Europeans had over the Africans.	
3. Note two factors within Africa that made it vulnerable to European conquest.	
The Division of Africa	
4. Note two outcomes of the Berlin Conference in 1884 and 1885.	
5. Note three groups that clashed over territory and resources in South Africa.	
6. Note one outcome of the Boer War.	

The Age of Imperialism

Imperialism in Africa

Key Terms and People

paternalism governing in a "parental" way by providing for needs but not giving rights

assimilation absorbing colonized people into the culture of the imperialist nation

Menelik II leader of Ethiopian resistance

Before You Read

In the last lesson, you learned about the reasons for imperialism in Africa.

In this lesson, you will read about how the colonies were controlled.

As You Read

Take notes to answer questions about European imperialism in Africa.

A NEW PERIOD OF IMPERIALISM; A BRITISH COLONY
What forms and methods did imperialist nations use to control their colonies?

Each imperial power had goals for its colonies. Imperialist nations had four forms of control: colonies, protectorates, spheres of influence, and economic imperialism.

A colony is an area ruled by a foreign government. A protectorate runs its own daily affairs but is controlled by an imperialist nation. A sphere of influence is an area where an imperialist nation has exclusive economic rights. Economic imperialism refers to a situation where an independent nation is controlled by foreign businesses rather than foreign governments.

Imperialist nations also developed two basic methods to manage their colonies. France and other European nations used direct control. They felt native peoples could not handle the tough job of running a country. Instead, the imperialist power governed. This policy was called **paternalism.** The French also had a policy of **assimilation.** All colonial institutions were patterned after French institutions. The French hoped that the native peoples would learn French ways.

Britain used a system of indirect control. In this system, local rulers had power over daily matters. There were also councils of native people and government officials. These councils were supposed to help native people learn to govern themselves in the British method.

When the United States began to colonize, it also used the indirect method of control.

Britain tried to rule Nigeria through indirect control. The British let local chiefs manage their areas. The system did not always work. The local chiefs in some regions of Nigeria resented having their power limited by the British.

1. What forms and methods did imperialists use to control and manage colonies?

_____

_____

_____

AFRICAN RESISTANCE
How did Africans resist imperialism?

Some Africans resisted imperialism. People in Algeria fought against the French for almost 50 years. In German East Africa, thousands of Africans died when they tried to use magic to fight German machine guns.

Only Ethiopia resisted the Europeans successfully. There, Emperor **Menelik II** played one European country against another. In 1896, he used European weapons to defeat an Italian army.

2. Who resisted imperialism in Africa, and what were the results?

_____

_____

THE LEGACY OF COLONIAL RULE
How did colonial rule affect Africa?

Africans enjoyed some benefits from colonial rule. European governments reduced local conflicts. The Europeans also brought Africa deeper into the world economy. Railroads, dams, and telephone and telegraph lines were built.

But imperialism mostly caused damage. Africans lost control over much of their land. Many African traditions were destroyed. People were forced out of their homes. Many were made to work in bad conditions. The boundaries that Europeans drew had no relation to ethnic divisions in Africa. These boundaries caused problems when the colonies became independent nations.

3. What were three benefits and three problems of colonial rule?

_____

_____

Lesson 2, *continued*

As you read this lesson, take notes to answer the questions.

European nations used various forms of colonial control.	
1. How did the British control Nigeria and other British colonies?	
2. What method of management did the French use with their colonies?	
African societies tried to resist European attempts at colonization.	
3. How did Algeria's resistance to French rule differ from the East Africans' resistance to German rule?	
4. Why was Ethiopia able to successfully resist European rule?	
European colonial rule greatly transformed African society.	
5. How did Africans benefit from colonial rule?	
6. What were the negative consequences of colonial rule for the African continent?	

The Age of Imperialism

Europeans Claim Muslim Lands

Key Terms and People

geopolitics interest in or taking of land for its location or products

Crimean War conflict in which the Ottoman Empire halted Russian expansion near the Black Sea

Suez Canal human-made waterway connecting the Red Sea and Mediterranean

Before You Read

In the last lesson, you read about imperialism in Africa.

In this lesson, you will learn about imperialism in Muslim lands.

As You Read

Use a diagram to note details that explain the decline of the Muslim states.

OTTOMAN EMPIRE LOSES POWER
***When* did the Ottoman Empire become weak?**

The Ottoman Empire was based in modern Turkey. But it controlled lands in eastern Europe, north Africa, and southwest Asia.

This empire lasted for hundreds of years, but by the 1800s, it was weak. The ruling party broke up into quarreling factions. Corruption and theft caused financial chaos. The Ottomans had once embraced modern technologies but now were falling behind the Europeans.

Nationalism began to stir among people in the empire. In 1830, Greece won its independence and Serbia won the right to govern itself. European nations eyed what remained of the empire hungrily.

1. What happened when the Ottoman Empire weakened?

_____

_____

EUROPEANS GRAB TERRITORY
***Where* did Europeans grab territory?**

Geopolitics is the interest in or taking of land for its location or products. It played an important role in the fall of the Ottoman Empire. Russia hoped to win control of the Black Sea so it could ship grain into the Mediterranean Sea. Russia fought a war with the Ottomans in the 1850s called the **Crimean War.**

Russia lost the war when Britain and France joined on the side of the Ottomans. Still, the Ottomans later lost

Lesson 3, *continued*

almost all of their land in Europe and parts of Africa. Muslim leaders, seeing this decline, decided to modernize their countries.

Russia also fought Great Britain in a war known as the "Great Game." Russia sought to extend its empire and gain access to India, one of Britain's most valuable colonies. The British defended India and also attempted to spread their empire beyond India's borders. Much of the war was fought in the independent Muslim kingdom of Afghanistan. After decades of fighting, both countries withdrew and agreed to respect Afghanistan's independence.

2. Why did Russia engage in the Crimean War and the Great Game?

_____

_____

EGYPT INITIATES REFORMS; PERSIA PRESSURED TO CHANGE
What **measures did Muslim countries take to avoid imperialist domination?**

Some Muslim leaders tried to adopt reforms to block European control of their lands. In Egypt, Muhammad Ali broke away from Ottoman control. He reformed the army and the economy. Ali's grandson continued to modernize the empire. He joined with the French in building the **Suez Canal.** It connected the Mediterranean to the Red Sea.

The canal was extremely expensive to build. Egypt quickly found that it could not afford to repay the money it owed. The British took control of the canal. Later the British took over the rest of the country as well.

In Persia, the Russians and the British competed for control. Russia wanted to use Persia to gain access to the Persian Gulf and Indian Ocean. Twice Russia forced Persia to give up territories through military victories.

Britain wanted to use Afghanistan as a buffer between India and Russia. In 1857, Britain forced Persia to give up all claims to Afghanistan.

In the early 1900s, oil was discovered in Persia. A British company signed an agreement with Persia's ruler to develop these oil fields. Persians rebelled against their ruler, who was corrupt, and the growing influence of Europeans. Then Russia and Britain stepped in and took control of the land.

In Muslim lands, the Europeans gained control by using economic imperialism and creating spheres of influence. Some Muslim countries tried to modernize. But these efforts came too late to prevent Europeans from taking over.

3. What happened in Egypt and in Persia?

_____

_____

Name _____ Class _____ Date _____

Lesson 3, *continued*

As you read this lesson, explain how each of the factors listed contributed to the decline of Muslim states.

1. Death of Suleyman I →	
2. Rise of nationalism →	
3. Geopolitics →	
4. Construction of the Suez Canal →	
5. Discovery of oil in Persia →	

The Age of Imperialism

British Imperialism in India

Key Terms and People

sepoy Indian soldier under British command

"jewel in the crown" term referring to India as the most valuable of all British colonies

Sepoy Mutiny uprising of Indian soldiers against the British

Raj British rule over India from 1757 to 1947

Before You Read

In the last lesson, you saw how Europeans grabbed Muslim lands.

In this lesson, you will read about British control of India.

As You Read

Use a diagram to take notes on causes and effects of British imperialism in India.

BRITISH EXPAND CONTROL OVER INDIA
How did British rule affect India?

The Mughal Empire of India fell into decline in the early 1700s. By the mid-1700s, the British East India Company was the most important power in India. The company held huge amounts of land. The company even had its own army. This army was led by British officers. It was staffed by **sepoys,** or Indian soldiers.

India was the main supplier of raw materials for Britain. The British called India the **"jewel in the crown"** because it was Britain's most valuable colony.

India enjoyed some benefits from British rule. India's rail system was the third largest in the world. The railroad helped make India's economy more modern. The British made other improvements, too. They built telephone and telegraph lines, dams, bridges, and canals. They also improved sanitation and public health and built schools.

But British rule also caused problems. A great deal of wealth flowed from India to Britain. Indian industry died out because of British trade laws. Many farmers and villages could no longer feed themselves because they were forced to grow cash crops. India suffered famines in the late 1800s. In addition, most British officials had racist attitudes that threatened Indian culture.

1. What problems did British rule bring?

_____

_____

THE SEPOY MUTINY
Why did Indians rebel?

By the mid-1800s, many Indians resented British rule. Many believed that the British wanted to convert them to Christianity. They also felt that the British treated them badly.

In 1857, some Indian soldiers heard rumors about British weapons. The rumors offended the Indians' religious feelings. The British handled the situation badly. The Indian soldiers rebelled. This rebellion has been called the **Sepoy Mutiny.** Fierce fighting took place between the sepoys and the British. It took the East India Company and British troops a year to put it down.

The Sepoy Mutiny failed because the Indians were divided. Muslims and Hindus did not trust each other. The Muslims wanted the Muslim Mughal Empire restored. Many Hindus preferred British rule to Muslim rule.

After the revolt, the British government took direct control of British India. The term **Raj** refers to British rule over India from 1857 to 1947.

2. What was the Sepoy Mutiny?

_____

_____

Lesson 4, *continued*

As you read about imperialism in India, briefly note the cause or effect (depending on which is missing) of each situation.

Causes	Effects
1.	The East India Company gained control of india.
2. The British established a railroad network in india.	
3.	Villagers were no longer self-sufficient; food production declined and famine set in.
4. The Sepoy Mutiny occurred and the uprising spread over much of northern India.	
5.	Indians formed the Indian National Congress and then the Muslim League, which eventually called for self-government.
6. The British partitioned Bengal into Hindu and Muslim sections.	

The Age of Imperialism

European Claims in Southeast Asia

Key Terms and People

Pacific Rim southeast Asian mainland and islands along the rim of the Pacific Ocean

King Mongkut king who helped Siam modernize

Before You Read

In the last lesson, you learned how the Indians reacted to British imperialism.

In this lesson, you will read about imperialism in southeast Asia.

As You Read

Use a diagram to write notes about the colonization of southeast Asia.

EUROPEAN POWERS INVADE THE PACIFIC RIM
Which Western powers grabbed land in southeast Asia?

European nations also grabbed land in the **Pacific Rim,** southeast Asia and the islands on the edge of the Pacific Ocean. The lands of southeast Asia were perfect for plantation agriculture. Sugar, coffee, cocoa, rubber, coconuts, bananas, and pineapples were important products.

The Dutch controlled Indonesia. Many of the Dutch who moved to Indonesia thought of Indonesia as their home. They set up a class system that kept the Dutch at the top. Wealthy and educated Indonesians came next. Plantation workers were at the bottom. The Dutch forced farmers to use one-fifth of their land for export crops.

The British took the port of Singapore plus Malaysia and Burma (modern Myanmar). They used

Singapore as a base for trade. It became one of the world's busiest ports. The British encouraged the Chinese to move to Malaysia. The Malaysians have become a minority in their own country. Tension between the Malays and the Chinese remains to this day.

France grabbed Indochina (modern Laos, Cambodia, and Vietnam). The French ruled Indochina directly and tried to push French culture on the Indochinese. The French did not encourage industry. Rice became a major crop. Although the Vietnamese grew more rice than before, they ate less of it because so much rice was sent out of the region. This problem set the stage for Vietnamese resistance to French rule.

Colonialism brought some features of modern life to these regions. But economic change benefited Europeans more than the local people. Even so, schooling, health, and sanitation were improved. Millions of people migrated

Lesson 5, *continued*

to new regions of southeast Asia. But the mix of cultures did not always go smoothly. Even today, some conflict between groups results from this period.

1. What major problems did colonialism bring?

   _____

   _____

SIAM REMAINS INDEPENDENT
How did imperialism affect Siam?

One land—Siam (modern Thailand)—stayed independent. Siam was surrounded by lands taken by the French and British. The French and British each did not want the other to control Siam. The Siamese kings played the French and British against one another to remain free of both nations.

King Mongkut and his son modernized Siam. They started schools and reformed the government. They also built railroads and telegraph lines and ended slavery. These changes happened with little social turmoil.

2. How did Siam confront imperialism?

   _____

   _____

Lesson 5, *continued*

As you read about the colonization of southeast Asia, write notes about each group.

1. Dutch East India Company		
Lands claimed	Major products	Impact of colonization

2. British		
Lands claimed	Immigration policy	Impact of colonization

3. French		
Lands claimed	Method of management	Impact of colonization

Guided Reading Workbook

The Age of Imperialism

U.S. Economic Imperialism

Key Terms and People

annexation addition of territory

Queen Liliuokalani last Hawaiian ruler of Hawaii

caudillo military dictator

Monroe Doctrine U.S. statement of opposition to European influence

José Martí Cuban writer who fought for Cuban independence

Spanish–American War war fought between the United States and Spain in 1898, in which the Americans supported the Cuban fight for independence

Emilio Aguinaldo Filipino nationalist who fought against the Americans

Panama Canal man-made waterway connecting the Atlantic and Pacific Oceans

Roosevelt Corollary statement that the United States had the right to exercise "police power" in the Western Hemisphere

Before You Read

In the last lesson, you read about European imperialism in Asia.

In this lesson, you will read about U.S. economic imperialism in Hawaii and Latin America.

As You Read

Answer questions about the major events in U.S. involvement in Latin America.

U.S. IMPERIALISM IN THE PACIFIC ISLANDS; LATIN AMERICA AFTER INDEPENDENCE
What lands did the United States acquire?

American businessmen grew wealthy from sugar plantations in Hawaii. But they wanted to make more money. They asked for the **annexation,** or addition, of Hawaii to the United States. That way they would get more money when they sold sugar in the United States.

In the 1890s, **Queen Liliuokalani** tried to regain control of her country for the Hawaiian people. The American businessmen overthrew her. They declared a republic. In 1898, Hawaii became a territory of the United States.

In the early 1800s, the new nations of Latin America had serious problems. Most people were poor laborers. Another problem was political unrest. Local military leaders who wanted power ruled Latin American nations as **caudillos,** or military dictators.

Lesson 6, *continued*

Landowners kept the caudillos in power. The landowners refused to give power to the poor people. Only people with property could vote.

Sometimes reformers did take office. But they never lasted long. When their reforms threatened the power of the wealthy too much, a dictator would rise and remove them from office.

1. What problems did the people in the new nations of Latin America face?

_____

_____

ECONOMIES GROW UNDER FOREIGN INFLUENCE
What nations controlled Latin American economies?

Latin America did not develop its own manufacturing industries. It had to import manufactured goods. These goods cost more than what was earned from exports.

In addition, Latin American countries often borrowed money from foreign banks. When they could not repay the loans, lenders took control of the businesses.

2. Why was Latin America's need to import goods a problem?

_____

_____

A LATIN AMERICAN EMPIRE
How did the United States gain Latin American territories?

In 1823, President James Monroe issued the **Monroe Doctrine.** It warned European nations against interfering in the American continents.

In the 1890s, the people of Cuba were fighting for their independence from Spain. The writer **José Martí** was one of them. The United States fought against Spain in the **Spanish–American War.**

After the Spanish–American War in 1898, the United States took control of Puerto Rico, Guam, and the Philippine Islands.

Filipino nationalists led by **Emilio Aguinaldo** fought against the Americans for their freedom. The United States defeated the rebels but promised to give the Philippines self-rule later. In the meantime, American businesses took advantage of Filipino workers.

Into the early part of the 20th century, Americans wanted to find a quicker route from the east to west coasts. They hoped to build a canal across Panama.

President Roosevelt offered $10 million to Colombia—to which Panama belonged—for the right to build this canal. When Colombia asked for more money, the United States helped the people of Panama revolt for independence. In return, the United States won a ten-mile-wide zone in Panama in which to build the **Panama Canal.** The canal opened in 1914.

In 1904, Roosevelt extended the Monroe Doctrine. He said that the United States had the right to act as "an international police power" in the Western Hemisphere. This statement is known as the **Roosevelt Corollary.**

3. How did the United States win a zone in Panama for a canal?

_____

_____

As you read this lesson, answer the questions about three factors that
set the stage for economic imperialism in Latin America.

Factor 1: Legacy of Colonial Rule	
1. In what ways did landowners "enslave" peasant workers?	
2. How was land distributed during colonial times?	
3. What political problems did independent nations face as a result of European colonial rule?	
Factor 2: Foreign Trade	
4. How did advances in technology affect Latin American trade?	
5. How did foreign countries gain control of Latin American industries?	
6. Why did Latin American nations remain poor and unindustrialized after they gained independence?	
Factor 3: "The Colossus of the North"	
7. Why did President Monroe issue the Monroe Doctrine?	
8. How did the Spanish–American War make the United States the dominant imperial power in Latin America?	
9. How did the United States expand its influence in Latin America in the early 1900s?	

Transformations Around the Globe

China Resists Outside Influence

Key Terms and People

Opium War war between Britain and China over the opium trade

extraterritorial rights rights of foreign residents to follow the laws of their own government rather than those of the host country

Taiping Rebellion rebellion against the Qing Dynasty

sphere of influence area in which a foreign nation controls trade and investment

Open Door Policy policy proposed by the United States giving all nations equal opportunities to trade in China

Boxer Rebellion rebellion aimed at ending foreign influence in China

Before You Read

In the last lesson, you read about U.S. imperialism in Hawaii and Latin America.

In this lesson, you will see how China dealt with foreign influence.

As You Read

Use a chart to identify the causes and effects of problems faced by China in the 1800s and early 1900s.

CHINA AND THE WEST
Was China able to resist foreign influence?

In the late 1700s, China had a strong farming economy based on growing rice. Other crops, such as peanuts, helped to feed its large population. The Chinese made silk, cotton, and ceramics. Mines produced salt, tin, silver, and iron. China needed nothing from the outside world.

China limited its trade with European powers. All goods shipped to China had to come through one port. Britain bought so much Chinese tea that it was eager to find something that the Chinese would want in large quantities. In the early 1800s, the British began shipping opium, a dangerous drug, to China. The opium came mostly from India. The Chinese tried to make the British stop.

As a result of the **Opium War** that followed, the British took possession of Hong Kong. Later, the United States and European nations won **extraterritorial rights** and the right to trade in five ports. The Chinese resented these treaties but could not stop them.

1. What happened as a result of the Opium War?

_____

_____

GROWING INTERNAL PROBLEMS
What problems did China face?

China had internal problems as well. The population had grown quickly. When rains were too light or too heavy, millions starved. The Chinese government was weak and too corrupt to solve its problems.

A leader arose who hoped to save China. His name was Hong Xiuquan, and he led the **Taiping Rebellion.** More than one million peasants joined his army. The rebels won control of large parts of the south. It took the government 14 years to put down this rebellion. The fighting destroyed much farmland. At least 20 million people died.

2. What was the Taiping Rebellion?

_____

_____

FOREIGN INFLUENCE GROWS
What was the official attitude toward reform?

In the late 1800s, one person ruled China—the Dowager Empress Cixi. She supported a few reforms in education, civil service, and the military. Despite her efforts to bring change, China continued to face problems.

Other countries were well aware of China's weakness, and they took advantage of the situation. Throughout the late 1800s, many foreign nations in Europe as well as Japan won **spheres of influence** in China. A sphere of influence is a region in which a foreign nation controls trade and investment.

The United States opposed these spheres of influence. Americans urged an **Open Door Policy,** in which all

powers had equal access to Chinese markets. The Europeans agreed. This policy did not help China, however.

3. How did foreigners begin to gain control over China?

_____

_____

AN UPSURGE IN CHINESE NATIONALISM
What actions resulted from growing nationalism?

Humiliated by their loss of power, many Chinese wanted strong reforms. In 1898, the young Emperor Guangxu, Cixi's nephew, tried to put in place broader reforms.

Conservatives didn't like this. The retired Empress Cixi took back control of the government.

Some Chinese peasants and workers formed the Society of Harmonious Fists, known as the Boxers. They wanted to get rid of all Western influence. That included any Chinese who had accepted Western culture or Christianity.

At the start of the **Boxer Rebellion** in early 1900, Boxers surrounded Beijing's European section. They were driven out by a multinational army.

Cixi finally began to allow major reforms. But change came slowly. In 1908, Chinese officials said that China would become a constitutional monarchy by 1917. However, unrest soon returned.

4. What was the Boxer Rebellion?

_____

_____

Lesson 1, *continued*

As you read this lesson, note some of the causes and effects of events
and policies that affected China.

Causes	Events/Policies	Effects
	1. Opium War	
	2. Taiping Rebellion	
	3. Self-strengthening movement	
	4. Open Door Policy	
	5. Boxer Rebellion	

Modernization in Japan

Key Terms and People

Treaty of Kanagawa treaty between the United States and Japan opening trade between the two nations

Meiji era period of rule by Emperor Mutsuhito from 1867 to 1912

Russo–Japanese War war between Russia and Japan fought in 1904

annexation addition of territory

Before You Read

In the last lesson, you read about foreign influence in China.

In this lesson, you will learn about the steps taken by Japan to modernize.

As You Read

Use a timeline to answer questions about steps Japan took toward modernization and its growth as an imperialistic power.

JAPAN ENDS ITS ISOLATION
How did isolation end in Japan?

From the early 1600s to the mid-1800s, Japan traded with China and the Dutch and had diplomatic contact with Korea. But beyond that, Japan was largely isolated. British, French, Russian, and American officials tried to convince the Japanese to open up. But the Japanese repeatedly refused.

That situation changed in 1853 when American steamships with cannons entered Japanese waters. The next year, Japan and the United States signed the **Treaty of Kanagawa.** It agreed to open Japan to trade with America. Soon afterwards, Japan made similar deals with European nations.

Many Japanese were upset with the shogun, the military dictator, who had

agreed to these new treaties. The Emperor Mutsuhito got their support and managed to overthrow the shogun. For the first time in centuries, the emperor ruled Japan directly. He reigned for 45 years, from 1867 to 1912. This period is called the **Meiji era.** The name Meiji means "enlightened rule."

The emperor wanted to modernize Japan. He sent government officials to Europe and the United States. From what they saw, they shaped a new Japan. They modeled the government after the strong central government of Germany. They patterned the army after Germany's and the navy after Britain's. They adapted the American system of schooling for all children.

The emperor also supported changes to Japan's economy. The country mined coal and built railroads and factories. In just a few years, Japan's economy was as modern as any in the world.

1. What steps did Emperor Mutsuhito take to modernize Japan?

_____

_____

IMPERIAL JAPAN
How did Japan increase its influence in Asia?

By 1890, Japan had the strongest military in Asia. It asked foreigners to give up their special rights in Japan. The European nations agreed. Japan felt equal to the Western nations.

Japan became more imperialistic as its power grew. When China broke an agreement not to send armies into Korea, Japan went to war. It drove China out of Korea and gained Taiwan and some other islands as new colonies. In 1904, Japan and Russia fought the **Russo–Japanese War** over China's Manchurian territory. Japan surprised the world by defeating a larger power that was supposed to be stronger.

The next year, Japan attacked Korea. Japan made Korea a protectorate. Japanese officials took more and more power away from the Korean government. The Korean king was unable to get help for his government from other countries. By 1910, Japan achieved **annexation** of Korea.

The Japanese were harsh rulers. They shut down Korean newspapers. They allowed only Japanese history and language to be taught. They took land from Korean farmers and gave it to Japanese settlers. They built factories run by Japanese only. Koreans were not allowed to start new businesses. Koreans resented these actions. They began a nationalist movement and protested against Japanese rule.

2. How did Japan expand its empire to Korea?

_____

_____

As you read about the modernization of Japan, answer the questions about the timeline.

1853	**Matthew Perry arrives in Tokyo harbor.**	1. What was the American motive in sending the fleet?
1854	**Japan signs the Treaty of Kanagawa.**	2. How did the United States benefit from the terms of the treaty?
1867	**Mutsuhito establishes a new government.**	3. What steps did the Meiji take to modernize Japan?
1885	**Japan and China pledge not to send armies into Korea.**	4. Why were both countries interested in Korea?
1894	**Sino–Japanese war begins.**	5. How did the war begin?
		6. What consequences did the war have?
1904	**Russia and Japan go to war over Manchuria.**	7. What was the cause of this war?
		8. What were some consequences?
1910	**Japan annexes Korea.**	9. How did the Japanese rule Korea?

Turmoil and Change in Mexico

Key Terms and People

Antonio López de Santa Anna leader in Mexico's fight for independence

Benito Juárez leader of *La Reforma*

La Reforma movement in Mexico aimed at achieving land reform, better education, and other goals

Porfirio Díaz dictator who came to power after Juárez

Francisco Madero enemy of Díaz who believed in democracy

"Pancho" Villa popular leader of the Mexican revolution

Emiliano Zapata leader of a powerful revolutionary army

Before You Read

In the last lesson, you read about Japanese imperialism.

In this lesson, you will read about revolution and reform in Mexico.

As You Read

Use a chart to compare the major accomplishments of the Mexican leaders discussed in this lesson.

SANTA ANNA AND THE MEXICAN WAR

Who was Santa Anna?

Antonio López de Santa Anna was a leading figure in the early history of independent Mexico. He fought for Mexican independence from Spain in 1821. He fought against Spain again in 1829 when Spain tried to recapture Mexico. He served as Mexico's president four times.

But in the 1830s, Santa Anna was unable to stop Texas from winning independence from Mexico. In the 1840s, the United States annexed Texas. This angered many Mexicans.

When a border dispute between Mexico and Texas turned into armed conflict, the United States invaded Mexico. Santa Anna led his nation's army and was defeated. Mexico surrendered huge amounts of land to the United States.

1. What losses did Mexicans suffer under Santa Anna?

_____

_____

Lesson 3, *continued*

JUÁREZ AND *LA REFORMA*
What was *La Reforma?*

Another important leader of the middle 1800s was **Benito Juárez.** Juárez wanted to improve conditions for the poor.

He led a movement called *La Reforma*—"the reform." *La Reforma* aimed to break the power of the large landowners and give more schooling to the poor. Juárez and his supporters won control of the government in 1858.

But conservatives who opposed *La Reforma* did not give up. They plotted with France to retake Mexico. In 1862, Napoleon III of France sent an army that captured the country in 18 months. Napoleon III named a European noble as emperor. But Juárez and his followers kept fighting. Five years later, they drove the French from Mexican soil and executed the emperor.

2. How did conservatives oppose *La Reforma?*

_____

_____

PORFIRIO DÍAZ AND "ORDER AND PROGRESS"
Who was Porfirio Díaz?

Juárez again pressed for his reforms. He made some progress but was ousted by a noted general named **Porfirio Diaz.** Porfirio Díaz was a leader in Mexican politics for more than 30 years. Díaz brought order to the country. He brought some economic growth, but he limited political freedom.

3. What were the benefits and drawbacks of Díaz's rule?

_____

_____

REVOLUTION AND CIVIL WAR
Who were Villa and Zapata?

In the early 1900s, calls for reform got louder. A leader named **Francisco Madero** called for the overthrow of Díaz. Francisco **"Pancho" Villa** and **Emiliano Zapata** called for better lives for the poor. They raised armies and forced Díaz to step down. But political unrest continued. For many years, leaders struggled for power. In 1917, Mexico adopted a new constitution that survived all of the turmoil.

Conflict continued until a new political party gained control of Mexico in 1929. The Institutional Revolutionary Party (PRI) brought some peace and political stability to a troubled land.

4. What were the main goals of Villa and Zapata?

_____

_____

As you read this lesson, take notes to answer questions about
revolution and reform in Mexico.

What were the major accomplishments of each leader? What was the political legacy of each?	
1. Antonio López de Santa Anna	
2. Benito Juárez	
3. Porfirio Díaz	

What role did each of the following play in the Mexican Revolution?	
4. Francisco Madero	
5. Francisco "Pancho" Villa	
6. Emiliano Zapata	
7. Venustiano Carranza	

World War I

Marching Toward War

Key Terms and People

militarism glorifying war and preparing for it

Triple Alliance military agreement between Germany, Austria-Hungary, and Italy

Kaiser Wilhelm II emperor of Germany

Triple Entente military agreement among Britain, France, and Russia

Before You Read

In the last lesson, you read about turmoil and change in Mexico.

In this lesson, you will learn about the beginnings of World War I.

As You Read

Use a chart to answer questions about important details regarding the beginnings of World War I.

RISING TENSIONS IN EUROPE
Why didn't peace last in Europe?

Many people in Europe had joined groups to work for peace. However, developments would soon lead Europe into war.

One of those developments was nationalism—a deep feeling of attachment to one's own nation. This force helped unify the people of a country. It also created competition between countries.

By 1900, six nations were rivals for power in Europe. These nations, called the Great Powers, were Germany, Austria-Hungary, Great Britain, Russia, Italy, and France. They competed economically, and they competed for neighboring land.

Imperialism was another force that helped lead to war. France and Germany were each seeking to control parts of Africa. They almost came to war twice in the early 1900s. Mistrust was a huge problem.

The third factor leading to war was a growing arms race. Each country in Europe—except Great Britain—built a large army. Glorifying war and preparing for it is called **militarism.**

1. What were three factors leading to war?

_____

_____

TANGLED ALLIANCES
What caused countries to fear one another?

Growing rivalries led the nations to make military alliances. Prussia's chancellor, Otto von Bismarck, feared that France would want revenge for its defeat in the Franco-Prussian War. He set out to isolate France, forming the **Triple Alliance** with Austria-Hungary and Italy. He also signed a treaty with Russia.

Kaiser Wilhelm II of Germany did not want to share power with Bismarck. He forced Bismarck to resign and followed his own foreign policy. He let the agreement with Russia end. Russia soon allied itself with France. This alliance meant that Germany would have to fight enemies on its eastern and western borders if there were a war with either country. Wilhelm II then moved to make the German navy larger.

Great Britain grew alarmed. In response to Prussia's moves, it entered into the **Triple Entente** alliance with France and Russia. The six Great Powers had now formed two camps—Germany, Austria-Hungary, and Italy against Britain, France, and Russia.

2. What two groups of nations developed?

_____

_____

CRISIS IN THE BALKANS
What part did the Balkans play in the increasing tensions?

Meanwhile, trouble was brewing in the Balkans, in southeastern Europe. The Ottoman Empire controlled this area. But it was breaking apart. Some peoples had formed new nations, while others hoped to do so. And both Austria-Hungary and Russia hoped to gain influence in the area.

Serbia was one new country. It wanted to bring other Slavic peoples who lived in the Balkans under its control. In 1908, Austria-Hungary seized Bosnia and Herzegovina. These lands had Slavic peoples. This action angered the Serbs. Tensions between Serbia and Austria rose steadily. Serbia vowed to take Bosnia and Herzegovina from Austria-Hungary, which vowed to oppose any such effort.

In June 1914, a Serbian killed Archduke Franz Ferdinand, the heir to the throne of Austria-Hungary. Austria-Hungary declared war on Serbia. Russia, also Slavic, came to Serbia's defense. Soon most of Europe would be at war.

3. How were the Serbians involved in the start of World War I?

_____

_____

Lesson 1, *continued*

As you read this lesson, answer the questions below about the situations and events that led to war in Europe.

a. What is it? b. How did it increase tensions among European nations?	
1. Nationalism	a. b.
2. Imperialism	a. b.
3. Militarism	a. b.
4. Triple Alliance (1882)	a. b.
5. Triple Entente (1907)	a. b.
6. Assassination in Sarajevo	a. b.

World War I

Europe Plunges into War

Key Terms and People

Central Powers Germany, Austria-Hungary, and other nations who fought on their side

Allies Great Britain, France, Russia, and other nations who fought on their side

Western Front region of northern France where much fighting took place

Schlieffen Plan Germany's plan for winning the war on two fronts

trench warfare fighting from trenches dug in the battlefield

Eastern Front region along German-Russian border where much fighting took place

Before You Read

In the last lesson, you read how World War I began.

In this lesson, you will learn the details of this costly and tragic war.

As You Read

Use a chart to trace the cause-and-effect relationships that marked the beginning of World War I.

THE GREAT WAR BEGINS
How did so many nations become involved?

The system of alliances turned the war between Austria-Hungary and Serbia into a wider war. Russia moved against Austria-Hungary. It figured that Germany would support Austria-Hungary. So it moved troops against Germany as well. Germany declared war on Russia. Soon after, it also declared war on Russia's ally, France. Great Britain declared war on Germany.

Germany and Austria-Hungary were called the **Central Powers.** Bulgaria and the Ottoman Empire joined Germany and Austria-Hungary. France, Britain,

and Russia were called the **Allies.** They were later joined by Italy, which broke with Germany and Austria-Hungary.

1. Who were the Allies and Central Powers?

_____

_____

A BLOODY STALEMATE
What kind of warfare was used?

Germany had a plan for winning the war on two fronts. The first front would be in France: the **Western Front.** After defeating France, Germany planned to turn east to face Russia. This **Schlieffen**

Plan called for a rapid push through France, a quick defeat of that nation, and then an attack on Russia. After the German army moved almost to Paris, however, French defenses strengthened and stopped them in September 1914. Both sides became bogged down in a bloody stalemate. Soldiers dug deep trenches into the ground. **Trench warfare** began.

When soldiers left the trenches to storm enemy lines, they faced powerful new weapons. Machine guns, tanks, poison gas, and larger pieces of artillery killed hundreds of thousands of soldiers.

2. What was the war like on the Western Front?

_____

_____

THE BATTLE ON THE EASTERN FRONT
What happened on the Eastern Front?

The war on the **Eastern Front** showed more movement at first—but it was equally destructive. Russian armies attacked both Germany and Austria-Hungary. They had some early success but were driven back in both places. One reason was that Russia did not have a fully industrial economy. It could not keep troops supplied. Meanwhile, the other Allies were unable to ship supplies to Russian ports.

Still, Russia had a huge population and could send millions to war. The large Russian army provided a constant threat to Germany. This threat prevented Germany from putting its full resources against the Allies in the west.

3. What weaknesses and strengths did Russia have?

_____

_____

Name _____ Class _____ Date _____

As you read this lesson, note the effects of each of the actions or situations (causes) listed below.

Causes	Effects
1. Russia mobilizes along the German border.	
2. Germany declares war on France.	
3. The Allies defeat the Germans in September 1914.	
4. Machine guns, tanks, poison gas, and large artillery pieces are used in battles along the Western Front.	
5. Russian forces attack both Austria and Germany.	
6. The Allies are unable to ship war supplies to Russia's ports.	

A Global Conflict

Key Terms and People

unrestricted submarine warfare using submarines to sink any ship without warning

total war war in which countries use all their resources for the war

rationing control of the amounts and kinds of goods people can have

propaganda one-sided information designed to persuade

armistice agreement to stop fighting

Before You Read

In the last lesson, you read how World War I was fought in Europe.

In this lesson, you will learn how the war affected the world.

As You Read

Use a timeline to answer questions about the effects of World War I.

WAR AFFECTS THE WORLD
What other areas of the world were involved?

As the war dragged on, it spread beyond Europe. In Southwest Asia, the Allies hoped to take a part of the Ottoman Empire called the Dardanelles. The attack failed with great loss of life. Farther south, Arab nationalists fought the Ottoman Turks with the help of the British. Elsewhere in Asia, Japan took German colonies in China and the Pacific Ocean. India, a British colony, sent over a million soldiers to fight. European colonies in Africa also saw action. The Allies captured three of the four German colonies in Africa.

On the seas, the British used their strong navy to block all supplies from reaching Germany. The Germans

responded by increasing their submarine attacks on ships bringing food and supplies to the Allies. They used **unrestricted submarine warfare,** sinking any ship without warning.

When American ships were sunk and lives were lost, Americans grew angry. Then the British intercepted a secret message from Germany to Mexico. This message asked Mexico to ally itself with Germany. In return, Germany offered to help Mexico regain land lost to the United States. Finally, in April 1917, Congress declared war on Germany.

1. What areas outside of Europe were affected by the war?

   _____

   _____

Lesson 3, *continued*

WAR AFFECTS THE HOME FRONT
What happened on the home fronts?

By 1917, the war had already killed millions. It had drastically changed the lives of millions more—people at home as well as soldiers fighting on the fronts. It had become a **total war,** demanding all resources of the opposing countries.

Governments took control of factories. It told them what and how much to produce. Governments also used **rationing.** This limited how much food and goods people could buy so armies in the field would have needed supplies. Governments used **propaganda** to get support. They also took steps to stop dissent, or opposition to the war.

With so many men in the military, women played a growing role in the economies of the countries at war. They worked in factories, offices, and shops. They built planes and tanks, grew food, and made clothing. These changes had an impact on people's attitudes toward what kind of work women could do.

2. What were three ways that the war affected people's day-to-day lives?

_____

_____

THE ALLIES WIN THE WAR
Why did the Allies win?

In 1917, the United States entered the war. And Russia left it. Suffering during the war chipped away at the Russian people's support for the czar. In March, he stepped down. Russian armies refused to fight. Just months later, a new revolution broke out. Communists seized control of Russia and made a treaty with Germany.

In March 1918, Germany tried one final attack. Once again, the German army nearly reached Paris. But the soldiers were tired, and supplies were short. The Allies, with fresh American troops, drove the Germans back.

Bulgaria and the Ottoman Empire surrendered. In October, a revolution overthrew the emperor of Austria-Hungary. In November, Kaiser Wilhelm II was forced to step down in Germany. The new government signed an **armistice,** an agreement to stop fighting. On November 11, 1918, Europe was finally at peace.

3. What were the final problems that Germany and Austria-Hungary faced?

_____

_____

THE LEGACY OF THE WAR
What was the cost of the war?

World War I had a devastating effect on the world. As far as human costs, about 8.5 million soldiers had died. Another 21 million had been wounded. Countless civilians had suffered as well. The economies of the warring nations had suffered serious damage, too. Farms were destroyed, and factories were ruined. One estimate said the war had caused $338 billion in damage. The war also had an emotional cost. People felt all the suffering did not seem to have a purpose. The art and literature of the years after the war reflected a new sense of hopelessness.

4. Name one human, one economic, and one emotional cost of the war.

_____

_____

Lesson 3, *continued*

As you read about the effects of the war on countries throughout the world, make notes to answer questions related to the timeline.

Feb. 1915	Gallipoli campaign begins.	1. What was the purpose of the Gallipoli campaign?
Jan. 1917	Germany announces a policy of unrestricted submarine warfare.	
Feb. 1917	British intercept the Zimmermann note.	2. Why did the United States enter the war?
April 1917	The United States enters the war.	
Nov. 1917	Lenin seizes power in Russia.	3. Why did the czar's government collapse?
March 1918	Germany and Russia sign Treaty of Brest-Litovsk.	4. What did this treaty accomplish?
July 1918	Allies and Germans fight Second Battle of the Marne.	5. What was the significance of this battle?
Nov. 1918	World War I ends.	6. What events signaled the final defeat of the Central Powers?

World War I

A Flawed Peace

Key Terms and People

Woodrow Wilson president who proposed the Fourteen Points and represented the United States at Versailles

Georges Clemenceau France's premier and delegate at Versailles

Fourteen Points Wilson's plan for a just and lasting peace

self-determination allowing people to decide for themselves about what kind of government they want

Treaty of Versailles agreement at the end of World War I between Germany and the Allied Powers

League of Nations international group with the goal of keeping peace among nations

Before You Read

In the last lesson, you read how World War I spread and finally ended.

In this lesson, you will learn about the harsh peace that followed.

As You Read

Use a chart to record notes to answer questions about the settlement that ended World War I.

THE ALLIES MEET AND DEBATE
What decisions were made at Versailles?

Many nations sent delegates to the peace talks in Paris. The main leaders were **Woodrow Wilson** of the United States, **Georges Clemenceau** of France, and David Lloyd George of Britain. Germany and its allies and Russia were not present.

Wilson pushed for his peace plan called the **Fourteen Points.** He wanted to end secret treaties and alliances and give people **self-determination,** the right to form their own nation. He also hoped to set up a world organization that would police the actions of nations and prevent future wars.

Britain and especially France had different views. They had suffered greatly in the war. They wanted to punish Germany. After long debates, the leaders finally agreed on a peace settlement. It was called the **Treaty of Versailles** and was signed in June 1919.

The treaty called for a **League of Nations**—the world organization that Woodrow Wilson wanted. Germany and Russia were left out of the League. The treaty took away German land in

Lesson 4, *continued*

Europe and took away its colonies in Africa and the Pacific. Limits were placed on the size of Germany's armed forces.

Finally, Germany was given complete blame for the war. That meant it would have to make payments to the Allies for the damage caused.

1. How did the Treaty of Versailles affect Germany?

_____

_____

A TROUBLED TREATY
Who opposed the treaty?

Germany's former colonies were given to the Allies to govern until they decided which were ready for independence. Poland, Czechoslovakia, and Yugoslavia were all declared independent. Finland, Estonia, Latvia, and Lithuania—once

part of Russia—were made independent nations as well. The treaty also broke up the Ottoman Empire. The Ottomans kept control only of Turkey.

The treaty did not make a lasting peace. The United States Senate never approved the treaty or joined the League of Nations. Germans bitterly resented the treaty because it placed all the blame for the war on them. Colonial peoples in Africa and Asia were angry because the treaty did not make them independent. Japan and Italy were also upset by getting few territorial gains.

2. Which groups opposed the treaty, and why?

_____

_____

Name _____ Class _____ Date _____

Lesson 4, *continued*

As you read this lesson, take notes to answer the questions about the peace settlement that ended World War I.

Wilson's goal of achieving a just peace differed from the peace objectives of France and Britain.	
1. What were the guiding principles of Wilson's Fourteen Points?	
2. What were the concerns and aims of France and Britain?	

After heated debate and compromise, the Treaty of Versailles was signed.	
3. In what ways did the treaty punish Germany?	
4. How did the treaty change the world map?	
5. How was Wilson's Fourteenth Point incorporated into the treaty?	

The legacy of Versailles was one of bitterness and loss.	
6. Why did the United States reject the treaty?	
7. How did this rejection affect the League of Nations?	
8. Why did many countries feel bitter and cheated as a result of the treaty?	

Revolution and Nationalism

Revolutions in Russia

Key Terms and People

proletariat revolutionary term for workers

Bolsheviks group of revolutionaries led by Lenin

Lenin leader of the Bolsheviks and first ruler of the Soviet Union

Rasputin eccentric monk assassinated because of his corrupt influence on the Russian royal family

provisional government temporary government led by Alexander Kerensky

soviet local governing council

Communist Party a political party practicing the ideas of Karl Marx and Lenin

Joseph Stalin revolutionary leader who took control of the Communist Party after Lenin

Before You Read

In the last lesson, you read about the settlement that ended World War I.

In this lesson, you will learn about the revolutions in Russia that occurred during the war.

As You Read

Use a chart to take notes to answer questions about factors in Russia that helped lead to revolution.

CZARS RESIST CHANGE; RUSSIA INDUSTRIALIZES
What was life like in Russia?

In 1881, Czar Alexander II was killed by radical students. The new czar, Alexander III, stopped reforms. He cracked down on anyone who seemed to threaten his government. He also mistreated non-Russian peoples who lived within the Russian empire, especially Jews. Nicholas II, the son of Alexander III, continued his father's firm rule.

In the late 1800s, Russia started a buildup of industry. It quickly became a leading producer of steel. Russia also built the Trans-Siberian Railway—the longest continuous rail line in the world.

Working conditions were poor, wages were low, and children were forced to work. Workers, called the **proletariat** by revolutionaries, grew angry. Some revolutionary groups wanted to overthrow the government. Some followed the teachings of Karl Marx. One group—the **Bolsheviks**—was led by

Lenin. He fled Russia a few years later to wait to put forth his ideas.

1. Who were the Bolsheviks?

_____

_____

CRISES AT HOME AND ABROAD
What crises did Russia face?

In early 1905, the Russian army killed hundreds of hungry workers who had peacefully gathered to ask for relief. Strikes spread in protest. Nicholas was forced to allow some reforms to take place. He approved the creation of the Duma, Russia's first parliament.

The suffering of World War I was the final blow against the czar. As the war worsened, the czar lost control. Soldiers refused to fight, prices shot sky high, and people starved. Meanwhile, his wife fell under the influence of an odd monk named **Rasputin.** He spread corruption throughout the government.

2. What developments helped lead to the revolution?

_____

_____

THE MARCH REVOLUTION; THE BOLSHEVIK REVOLUTION
Who led the Bolshevik Revolution?

In March 1917, the czar was forced to step down. A year later, he and his family were executed. A **provisional government** led by Alexander Kerensky was formed. Kerensky hoped to keep Russia in the war. The decision cost him the support of soldiers who no longer wanted to fight. He also lost the support of workers and peasants who wanted an end to food shortages. Across the country, these forces formed local

councils called **soviets.** In the middle of all this, Lenin returned to Russia.

Lenin's slogan "Peace, Land, and Bread" was soon taken up by many people. In November 1917, armed workers took control of government offices. Kerensky's power ended.

To win the peasants' support, Lenin ordered all farmland be given to them. Workers were given control of the factories. Soon, Lenin agreed to a peace treaty with Germany. It gave away large amounts of Russian land, but it ended the war. Then, forces opposed to Lenin's revolution tried to defeat the Bolshevik army. The civil war lasted two years. The fighting and the famine that followed killed about 14 million Russians. In the end, Lenin's Red Army won.

3. Who fought the civil war?

_____

_____

LENIN RESTORES ORDER; STALIN BECOMES DICTATOR
How did Lenin bring back order?

In 1921, Lenin started a new plan to rebuild the Russian economy. It allowed for some private ownership of property. He also changed the government to form a new nation—the Soviet Union. It would be run by the leaders of the **Communist Party.** By the late 1920s, the Soviet economy had recovered. Farms and factories were producing as much as they had before World War I. After Lenin's death, **Joseph Stalin** took power.

4. What changes did Lenin make?

_____

_____

As you read this lesson, take notes to answer questions about some
factors in Russia that helped lead to revolution.

How did each of the following help to ignite the full-scale revolution?	
1. Policies of the czars	
2. Industrialization and economic growth	
3. The Russo–Japanese War	
4. "Bloody Sunday"	
5. World War I	
6. The March Revolution	
How did each of the following help the Bolsheviks gain and hold political control?	
7. November 1917 Revolution	
8. Civil war between the Red and White Armies	
9. Organization of Russia into republics	
What role did each of the following play in the Russian Revolution?	
10. Karl Marx	
11. V. I. Lenin	
12. Leon Trotsky	

Revolution and Nationalism

Totalitarianism

Key Terms and People

totalitarianism government that has total control over people's lives

Great Purge arrest, exile, or killing of thousands of suspected enemies of the Communist Party

command economy economy in which the government makes all the economic decisions

Five-Year Plan plan to develop the Soviet Union's economy

collective farm large, government-owned farm

Before You Read

In the last lesson, you learned about the factors leading to revolution in Russia.

In this lesson, you will read about the totalitarian government that resulted.

As You Read

Use a web diagram to list key characteristics of Stalin's totalitarian state.

A GOVERNMENT OF TOTAL CONTROL
What is totalitarianism?

The term *totalitarianism* describes a government that takes control of almost all parts of people's lives. A very powerful leader leads this type of government. Usually the leader brings security to the nation. The government stays in power by using different ways to keep control.

The weapons of totalitarianism include using police terror. Police may spy on people, use brutal force, or even murder them. The government might also control schools and use them to mold students' minds. Another weapon is propaganda. This is false information that is spread by the government to make people believe the government is working for their best interests. At other times the government will censor, that is block, certain information from becoming public.

Totalitarian rulers might also choose some people to persecute. The group may be blamed for things that go wrong in the country. Often these are people from a certain ethnic group or religion. They may be forced to live in certain areas or have rules that apply only to them.

Lesson 2, *continued*

1. What are two weapons of totalitarianism?

_____

_____

STALIN BUILDS A TOTALITARIAN STATE
How did Stalin control the country?

Stalin kept tight control on the Soviet Union. He did this by creating a powerful secret police. In the mid-1930s, he turned against enemies—both real and imagined—within the Communist Party. Thousands were arrested. Many were sent to exile or killed. This was known as the **Great Purge.**

Stalin also used propaganda to keep control. He controlled newspapers, radio, and other sources of information. He also used the arts to promote his ideas. In addition, Stalin's government moved against religion. Churches were destroyed. Church leaders were killed or sent into exile.

2. Who died in the Great Purge?

_____

_____

STALIN SEIZES CONTROL OF THE ECONOMY
How did Stalin change the economy?

Stalin built a **command economy.** This is an economy in which the government makes all the decisions about economic life. Stalin outlined **Five-Year Plans** to develop the economy. The plans focused on making the economy fully industrial.

All resources went to this effort. As a result, there were shortages of food, housing, and clothing for many years.

Stalin also began a farming revolution. The government took control of people's farms. It put them together into large, government-owned farms called **collective farms.** Wealthy peasants called kulaks resisted. Millions were killed, and millions more were exiled to Siberia. Stalin got farm output to rise by using these brutal methods.

3. How did Stalin's economic changes result in suffering?

_____

_____

DAILY LIFE UNDER STALIN; TOTAL CONTROL ACHIEVED
How did Stalin change Soviet society?

Stalin completely changed Soviet society. Women enjoyed equal rights. They filled all kinds of jobs on farms and in factories. They studied for careers that before had been closed to them. People, in general, were more educated.

By the mid-1930s, Stalin was in complete control of all economic and political affairs in the Soviet Union. The Soviet Union had been transformed into a major political and economic world power.

4. What benefits did Stalin's rule bring to women?

_____

_____

Lesson 2, *continued*

As you read this lesson, fill in the web diagram with key characteristics
of Stalinist Russia.

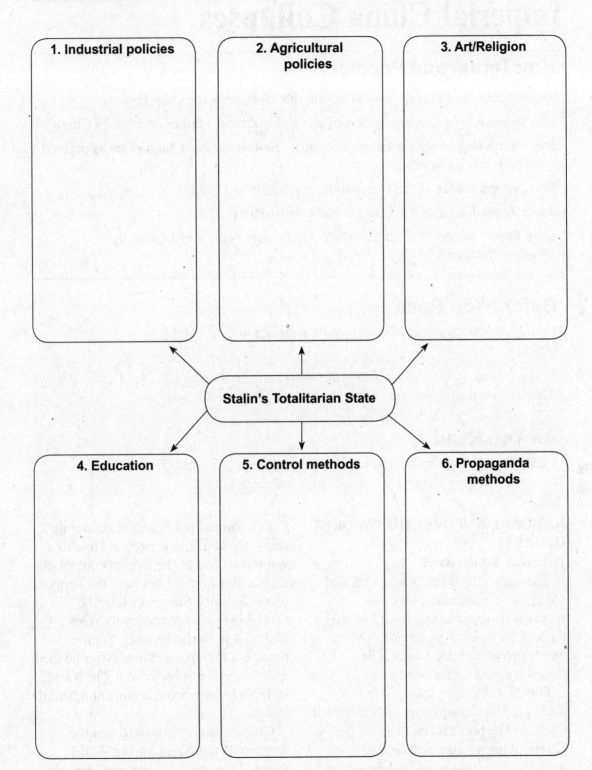

1. Industrial policies

2. Agricultural policies

3. Art/Religion

Stalin's Totalitarian State

4. Education

5. Control methods

6. Propaganda methods

Imperial China Collapses

Key Terms and People

Kuomintang Nationalist Party of China that overthrew the Qing Dynasty

Sun Yixian one of the first leaders of the Kuomintang; "father of modern China"

May Fourth Movement Chinese Nationalists protest against China's fate as decided by the Treaty of Versailles

Mao Zedong leader of the Communist revolution in China

Jiang Jieshi leader of the Chinese Nationalist Party

Long March escape of Communists to safety after being surrounded by Nationalist forces

Before You Read

In the last lesson, you read about totalitarianism in the Soviet Union.

In this lesson, you will learn about the overthrow of the Qing dynasty and the beginnings of the Communist Party in China.

As You Read

Use a chart to note cause-and-effect relationships in the struggle between Nationalist and Communist movements in China.

NATIONALISTS OVERTHROW QING DYNASTY
Who was Sun Yixian?

The early 20th century was a time of change in China. Many Chinese resented the great control that foreign nations had over their economy. Some wanted to modernize China. They hoped it could regain power.

One of the groups involved in this push was the **Kuomintang,** or Nationalist Party, led by **Sun Yixian.** In 1912, the Kuomintang overthrew the Qing dynasty. A republic was established, and Sun was made the president.

Sun wanted political and economic rights for all Chinese people. He also wanted an end to the foreign control of China. But Sun did not have the support of the military. Six weeks later, he turned over his presidency to Yuan Shikai, a powerful general. Yuan became a military dictator. After he died in 1916, civil war broke out. The people suffered terribly from famine and brutal attacks.

China's leaders hoped to win the support of the Allies during World War I. They declared war on Germany. When the war ended, though, they were disappointed. The Treaty of Versailles did not give China freedom from foreign influence. It only changed masters. The parts of China that had been controlled by Germany were handed over to Japan.

Angry Chinese protested during the **May Fourth Movement.** Among the protesters were workers, shopkeepers, and professionals. Some members of the movement looked to the success of communism in the Soviet Union as a model for China.

1. What did China's Nationalists want?

_____

_____

THE COMMUNIST PARTY IN CHINA
What happened to the Communist Party?

In the 1920s, revolutionaries organized the Chinese Communist Party. Among its leaders was a man named **Mao Zedong.** He later became the leader of China's Communist revolution.

Meanwhile, Sun Yixian became disappointed in the Western democracies. They refused to support his struggling government. He decided to become allies with the newly formed Communist Party. Sun sought Soviet help, too. He died in 1925. **Jiang Jieshi** became leader of the Kuomintang.

At first, Jiang joined with the Communists to try to defeat the warlords. These warlords ruled as much of the Chinese countryside as their armies could conquer. Together the Nationalists and Communists successfully fought the warlords.

Many in the Kuomintang were business people. They now feared Communist ideas about government control of economic life. In 1927, Jiang

began fighting the Communists. The Communists were forced into hiding. In 1928, Jiang became president of China. Soon China was torn by a civil war between the remaining Communists and Jiang's forces.

2. What role did Jiang Jieshi play in creating the civil war?

_____

_____

CIVIL WAR RAGES IN CHINA
Who fought the civil war?

Jiang had promised democracy and political rights to all Chinese. But his government had become less democratic and more corrupt. Nothing was done to improve the life of the rural peasants. Many of them gave their support to the Chinese Communist Party.

Communist leader, Mao Zedong, built an army of peasants. In 1933, Jiang's army surrounded them. But the Communists got away. They began the famous **Long March** of 6,000 miles to the north. Thousands died. The Communists settled in caves in Northwest China.

At the same time, China had other problems. In 1931, Japan invaded the part of China called Manchuria. Japan took control there and six years later began invading other areas. With this new threat, Jiang and the Communists agreed to unite temporarily to fight the Japanese.

3. What finally united Communist and non-Communist forces?

_____

_____

Lesson 3, *continued*

As you read this lesson, note some of the cause-and-effect relationships that marked the struggle between Nationalists and Communists in China.

Causes	Actions/Events	Effects
	1. Sun's Revolutionary Alliance overthrows the Qing dynasty.	
	2. Sun turns presidency over to Yuan Shikai.	
	3. The May Fourth Movement begins.	
	4. Nationalist forces move into Shanghai.	
	5. Communists begin the Long March.	
	6. Japan invades Manchuria.	

Revolution and Nationalism

Nationalism in Southwest Asia

Key Terms and People

Ottoman Empire an empire founded in 1299 and dissolved in 1922

Central Powers alliance including Germany, Austria-Hungary, and the Ottoman Empire that fought together in World War I

Mustafa Kemal leader of Turkish nationalists who overthrew the last Ottoman sultan

Before You Read

In the last lesson, you read about nationalism and civil war in China.

In this lesson, you will learn about nationalism in Southwest Asia.

As You Read

Use a chart to take notes to answer questions about the changes that occurred in Southwest Asia after World War I.

TURKISH NATIONALISM
***How* did World War I lead to change in Turkey?**

Modern-day Turkey had long been a part of the **Ottoman Empire.** The empire, centered in Constantinople (present-day Istanbul), had been in existence since around 1300 CE and was ruled as an absolute monarchy under a sultan.

By the late 19th century, reformers who became known as Young Turks began to challenge the Ottoman ruling system. During World War I, the Ottoman Empire joined Germany as part of the **Central Powers.** After the defeat of Germany and its allies, the Ottoman Empire was broken up. Only Turkey remained under Ottoman rule. In spite of reforms, however, resistance to the rule of the sultan continued.

In the 1920s, **Mustafa Kemal,** a military commander, led nationalists in overthrowing the last Ottoman sultan. Kemal became the leader of a new republic in Turkey. He modernized the society and the economy in Turkey. Among the reforms instituted were the separation of religious laws from the nation's laws, the granting of the vote to women, and the launching of government programs to spur industry and economic growth.

1. Who was Mustafa Kemal?

_____

_____

Lesson 4, *continued*

CHANGES IN SOUTHWEST ASIA
What further changes occurred in Southwest Asia after World War I?

The aftermath of World War I brought changes to Southwest Asia in addition to the founding of a new republic in Turkey. The weakened state of European countries allowed nationalist leaders throughout the area to establish new countries.

Before World War I, both Britain and Russia had influence in the ancient country of Persia. Britain tried to take control of all of Persia after the war. This led to a nationalist revolt. In 1921, Reza Shah Pahlavi, a Persian army officer, seized power. He later changed his country's name to Iran. As in Turkey, women gained new rights and the country began to modernize. Unlike in Turkey, modernization in Iran did not include democratic reforms.

In Arabia, different groups united to form one kingdom called Saudi Arabia. However, the rulers of Saudi Arabia, unlike those of Turkey and Iran, held on to Arab and Islamic traditions. Custom, religion, and family ties were the basis of society. There were no efforts to practice democracy.

Starting in the 1920s, Southwest Asia as a whole saw major economic change and development. Western companies discovered large reserves of oil in several countries in this area. Oil brought huge sums of money to these countries. Western nations tried to gain power in the region so they could get some of this wealth.

2. What new countries were formed in Southwest Asia?

_____

_____

Guided Reading Workbook

Name _____ Class _____ Date _____

As you read this lesson, take notes to answer the questions about the changes that occurred in Southwest Asia after World War I.

How did each of the following contribute to changes in Southwest Asia after World War I?	
1. the Ottoman Empire joining the Central Powers	
2. the weakened state of European powers	
3. the discovery of oil	
How did each country gain its independence?	
4. Turkey	
5. Persia	
6. Saudi Arabia	

Guided Reading Workbook

Postwar Uncertainty

Key Terms and People

Albert Einstein scientist who developed the theory of relativity

theory of relativity idea that as moving objects approach the speed of light, space and time become relative

Sigmund Freud physician who exposed the workings of the unconscious mind

existentialism philosophy that says each person must make meaning in a world that has no universal meaning

Friedrich Nietzsche German philosopher who dismissed reason, democracy, and progress as empty ideas

surrealism art movement in which a dreamlike world, outside of reality, is portrayed or evoked

jazz lively, loose form of popular music developed in the United States

Charles Lindbergh first person to fly alone across the Atlantic

Before You Read

In the last lesson, you read about nationalism in Southwest Asia.

In this lesson, you will learn how new ideas changed old ways of thinking.

As You Read

Use a chart to take notes to answer questions about new ideas and lifestyles that developed during the 1920s.

A NEW REVOLUTION IN SCIENCE
How did Einstein and Freud challenge old ideas?

The years after World War I were marked by both uncertainty and new ideas. Two thinkers challenged old ways of thinking. **Albert Einstein** changed physics with his ideas about space, time, matter, and energy. His **theory of relativity** said that as moving objects near the speed of light, space and time become relative. That means they

change. **Sigmund Freud** changed the way people thought about the human mind. He said that much of human behavior was irrational—due to urges and desires buried in the unconscious mind.

1. What were Einstein's and Freud's new ideas?

_____

_____

LITERATURE IN THE 1920S
How did writers and philosophers of the 1920s reflect society's concerns?

Many writers and philosophers lost faith in reason and progress after they looked at the destruction caused by World War I. Authors like Franz Kafka wrote about the horrors of modern life. His novels put people in threatening situations that they could not understand or escape.

Other thinkers developed the idea known as existentialism. **Existentialism** argues that there is no universal meaning to the world. Each person must give life meaning through his or her own actions. These thinkers had been influenced by **Friedrich Nietzsche.** Nietzsche was a German philosopher of the late 1800s. He said that reason, democracy, and progress were empty ideas. He urged people to adopt the values of pride and strength.

2. What is existentialism?

_____

_____

REVOLUTION IN THE ARTS
How was painting of this time different from traditional painting?

Artists rebelled against traditional painting. They did not re-create realistic objects. Paul Klee used bold colors and distorted lines. Pablo Picasso founded a style called cubism that broke objects into geometric shapes. An art movement called **surrealism** showed a dreamlike existence outside reality.

Composers created a new style of music. Some, like Igor Stravinsky, used unusual rhythms or harsh, rather than pleasing, sounds. African American musicians in the United States developed a lively, loose form of popular music called **jazz.**

3. What two new styles arose in the visual arts?

_____

_____

SOCIETY CHALLENGES CONVENTION; TECHNOLOGICAL ADVANCES IMPROVE LIFE
How did society change?

Society changed after World War I as well. Young people experimented with modern values. Women set aside earlier forms of dress, wearing new styles that were looser and shorter. Many women also began to work in new careers. Many African Americans left the South for northern cities to begin new lives.

Technology brought about changes to society as well. Improvements to the automobile helped make cars more desirable and affordable. More and more people bought cars. They began to move to suburbs. Another change was the growth in air travel. **Charles Lindbergh** flew alone across the Atlantic Ocean in 1927. In 1932, Amelia Earhart became the first woman to make the flight alone.

The radio was developed and became popular. In the 1920s, large radio networks were built. Soon millions of people were entertained by radios in their homes. Millions more went to movie theaters to watch motion pictures.

4. What major changes came about in travel and entertainment?

_____

_____

Name _____ Class _____ Date _____

Lesson 1, *continued*

As you read this lesson, take notes to answer questions about new ideas
and lifestyles that developed during the 1920s.

How did the following challenge deeply rooted ideas and traditions?			
1. Theory of relativity	2. Freudian psychology	3. Existentialism	4. Surrealism

How did the following demonstrate the independent spirit of the times?	
5. Jazz	6. Women

How did the following change ways of life?			
7. Automobiles	8. Airplanes	9. Radio	10. Movies

Years of Crisis

A Worldwide Depression

Key Terms and People

coalition government temporary alliance of several political parties

Weimar Republic government of Germany after World War I

Great Depression severe economic downturn that followed the collapse of the U.S. stock market in 1929

recession a slowdown in a nation's economy

Franklin D. Roosevelt president of the United States during the Depression

New Deal Roosevelt's program for creating jobs and improving the American economy

John Maynard Keynes British economist whose theory states that governments could prevent economic downturns through deficit spending

Before You Read

In the last lesson, you read about new ideas in the postwar world.

In this lesson, you will learn about economic crisis and worldwide depression.

As You Read

Use a chart to note reasons for major developments regarding postwar Europe and the global depression.

POSTWAR EUROPE; THE WEIMAR REPUBLIC
What problems did Europe face after the war?

After the war, European countries were in bad political and economic shape. Even nations that had democratic governments for many years experienced problems. They had so many political parties that no one party could rule alone. Sometimes a **coalition government** had to be formed. This was an alliance of several political parties. In addition, governments lasted for such a short time that it was hard to develop policies.

The situation was the worst in Germany. The people felt little loyalty to the government. Germany's government, the **Weimar Republic,** was very weak. Prices rose sharply, and money lost its value. Later, American bank loans helped the German economy recover.

World nations also took steps to try to make sure there would be lasting peace. France and Germany promised never to attack one another. Most countries of the world signed a treaty in which they pledged not to go to war. There was no way to enforce the treaty, however.

1. Why was the postwar situation in Germany especially bad?

_____

_____

FINANCIAL COLLAPSE; THE GREAT DEPRESSION
Where and how did the Great Depression begin?

The economy of the United States enjoyed a boom in the 1920s. But this growth hid problems. Consumers were unable to buy all the goods produced. When their purchases slowed, factories slowed production. Farmers faced falling food prices and slow sales. They were unable to repay loans and lost their farms. In 1929, stock prices in the United States plunged. The **Great Depression** had begun.

The Depression affected other countries. Nations raised tariffs—taxes on goods imported from other countries—to keep import prices high. They hoped to increase sales by local companies. Unfortunately, trade between nations dropped, and unemployment shot up in many countries. The world suffered.

2. What caused the Great Depression?

_____

_____

THE WORLD CONFRONTS THE CRISIS
How did various countries meet this crisis?

Each country met the **recession**, or economic slowdown, in its own way. In Britain, a new multiparty government took over. It took steps that slowly improved the economy and cut unemployment.

In France, the political situation was worse. After several governments lost support, moderates and socialists combined to form a government. It passed laws to help workers, but companies raised prices to cover their labor costs. Unemployment remained high.

In Sweden, Norway, and Denmark, the governments played active roles in the economy. They taxed people with jobs to have money to pay benefits to people without jobs. The governments also created jobs by hiring out-of-work people to build roads and buildings.

In the United States, **Franklin D. Roosevelt** began a program called the **New Deal.** The government spent large amounts of money on constructing roads, dams, bridges, airports, and buildings. This effort created jobs for millions. Businesses and farmers also got help from the government. The New Deal reflected policies advocated by the British economist **John Maynard Keynes,** who called for strong government action to counter economic troubles. The American economy got better, but the recovery was slow.

3. How did the United States deal with the crisis?

_____

_____

Name _____ Class _____ Date _____

As you read about postwar Europe and the global depression, note one
or more reasons for each of the following developments.

1. Postwar democracies saw frequent changes in government.	2. In Germany, the Weimar Republic was weak from the start.
3. Postwar Germany suffered from severe economic inflation.	4. The United States had a flawed economy.
5. On October 29, 1929, the U.S. stock market crashed.	6. A long depression followed the crash in the United States.
7. Collapse of the U.S. economy affected countries worldwide.	8. In Britain, the National Government rescued the economy.
9. In France, the Popular Front was formed as a coalition government.	10. Scandinavian countries dealt with the economic crisis successfully.

Guided Reading Workbook

Years of Crisis

Fascism Rises in Europe

Key Terms and People

fascism political movement based on nationalism that gives power to a dictator and takes away individual rights

Benito Mussolini fascist leader of Italy

Adolf Hitler fascist leader of Germany

Nazism German brand of fascism

Mein Kampf book by Hitler outlining his beliefs and goals for Germany

lebensraum living space

Before You Read

In the last lesson, you read about the Great Depression.

In this lesson, you will learn about the rise of fascism in Europe during troubled economic times.

As You Read

Use a chart to trace cause-and-effect relationships concerning the rise of fascism.

FASCISM'S RISE IN ITALY
Why did fascism arise in Italy?

The economic crisis of the Great Depression led to the loss of democracy in some countries. In these nations, millions of people turned to strong rulers to try to solve their economic problems. Such leaders followed a set of beliefs called **fascism.** Fascist leaders were very nationalistic. They believed in authority and built powerful military forces. Fascist governments were controlled by one party, and that party was ruled by one leader. The leader was the nation's dictator. Fascist governments did not let their people have individual rights.

Fascism arose in Italy. It started there because people were angry that they did not get more territory in the treaty that ended World War I. Also, inflation and unemployment were big problems. **Benito Mussolini** came to power by promising to help the economy and build the armed forces. He used armed thugs to threaten political opponents. The king of Italy decided Mussolini was the best hope to save his dynasty and let him lead the government.

Mussolini became Il Duce, or the leader, of Italy. He outlawed all political parties except fascism. He tried to control the economy and outlawed strikes.

Guided Reading Workbook

1. What did Mussolini promise the Italians?

_____

_____

HITLER RISES TO POWER IN GERMANY
How did Hitler gain control of Germany?

Another fascist came to power in Germany. **Adolf Hitler** was the leader of the Nazi party. The German brand of fascism was called **Nazism.** He tried to take control of the government of Germany in 1923, but the attempt failed. He was sent to prison. In prison, Hitler wrote a book that summarized his ideas. It was called *Mein Kampf.* Hitler believed that Germans were superior to all other people. He said that the Treaty of Versailles treated Germany unfairly. He also said that a crowded Germany needed more *lebensraum,* or living space. To get that space, he promised to conquer the lands of eastern Europe and Russia.

2. What were some of Hitler's beliefs?

_____

_____

HITLER BECOMES CHANCELLOR
What did Hitler do when he became Germany's leader?

When the Depression hit Germany, the country was in terrible shape. Hitler was named leader of the German government. Soon, he took the powers of a dictator. He became Germany's

führer, or leader. Those who opposed him were arrested. His economic program gave work to millions but took away their rights to organize into unions or to strike. He took control of all areas of life. He burned books that went against Nazi ideas. He forced children to join Nazi groups.

Hitler also attacked Germany's Jews. Laws took away their rights. In November 1938, mobs attacked Jewish people and destroyed thousands of Jewish-owned buildings. This was the start of a process to eliminate the Jews from German life.

3. What changes did Hitler make?

_____

_____

OTHER COUNTRIES FALL TO DICTATORS
What other countries were ruled by dictators?

Fascist dictators took control in other countries as well, including Hungary, Poland, Yugoslavia, Albania, Bulgaria, and Romania. All had dictators or kings who ruled like dictators. Only Czechoslovakia remained as a democracy in eastern Europe.

Elsewhere in Europe, only in nations with strong democratic traditions—Britain, France, and the Scandinavian countries—did democracy survive.

4. Why did democracy survive in some countries?

_____

_____

Lesson 3, *continued*

As you read about the rise of fascism, note causes and effects associated with each event.

Causes	Event	Effects
	1. Mussolini gains popularity.	
	2. King Victor Emmanuel III puts Mussolini in charge of the government.	
	3. Hitler is chosen leader of the Nazi party.	
	4. Hitler is tried for treason and sentenced to prison.	
	5. President Paul von Hindenburg names Hitler chancellor in 1933.	
	6. Hitler has books burned in huge bonfires.	
	7. Nazis pass laws depriving Jews of their rights.	

Years of Crisis

Aggressors Invade Nations

Key Terms and People

Hirohito emperor of Japan from 1926 to 1989; he led Japan during World War II

appeasement giving in to keep the peace

Axis Powers Germany, Italy, and Japan

Francisco Franco Spain's fascist dictator

isolationism belief that political ties with other countries should be avoided

Third Reich German empire

Munich Conference meeting of world powers in 1938 that allowed Hitler to take part of Czechoslovakia

Before You Read

In the last lesson, you read about the rise of fascism.

In this lesson, you will learn about military actions that led to a second world war.

As You Read

Use a timeline to trace incidents of military aggression in the 1930s.

JAPAN SEEKS AN EMPIRE
Why did Japan wish to expand?

Although Japan had become more democratic in the 1920s, military leaders took control of Japan during the Great Depression. They kept **Emperor Hirohito** as head of state, but they ruled in his name. The military leaders wanted to solve Japan's economic problems by foreign expansion.

In 1931, the Japanese army invaded Manchuria, a province of China. Manchuria was rich in coal and iron. These were valuable resources for the Japanese economy. Other countries spoke in protest in the League of

Nations but did nothing else. Japan ignored the protests. In 1933, it pulled out of the League.

Four years later, Japan invaded China. The powerful Japanese army swept Chinese fighters aside. It killed tens of thousands of civilians and soldiers in the city of Nanjing. In spite of these losses, Chinese forces—both the nationalists of the government and Communist rebels—continued to resist Japan.

1. What territories did Japan invade?

_____

_____

Lesson 4, *continued*

EUROPEAN AGGRESSORS ON THE MARCH
What European nations were aggressors?

Italy's Mussolini also wanted to expand. He dreamed of an Italian empire in Africa. In 1935, he ordered the invasion of Ethiopia. His troops won an easy victory. Haile Selassie, the emperor of Ethiopia, pleaded with the League of Nations to help. The League did nothing. By giving in to Mussolini in Africa, Britain and France hoped to keep the peace in Europe.

Hitler made moves also. He broke the Versailles Treaty by rebuilding Germany's army. In 1936, he sent troops into an area along the Rhine River between Germany and France that the treaty had forbidden the Germans to enter. The French and British responded with **appeasement**—giving in to keep the peace.

The German movement into the Rhineland marked a turning point in the march toward war. Also in 1936, Hitler signed an alliance with Mussolini and with Japan. These three nations came to be called the **Axis Powers.**

In 1936, civil war broke out in Spain. The army, led by General **Francisco Franco,** revolted against a government run by liberals and socialists. Hitler and Mussolini sent aid to the army, which was backed by Spanish fascists. The Soviet Union sent aid to the government. In early 1939, the government's resistance to the army collapsed. Francisco Franco became Spain's fascist dictator.

2. What places did Germany and Italy invade?

_____

_____

DEMOCRATIC NATIONS TRY TO PRESERVE PEACE
Why did the world's democracies fail to stop the aggression?

At this time, many Americans resisted a new role as a world leader. They believed that the United States should follow a policy of **isolationism,** avoiding political ties with other countries. This, it was thought, would keep the country out of another foreign war.

In March 1938, Hitler moved troops into Austria. He made it part of the **Third Reich,** or German Empire. This broke the Versailles Treaty again. France and Britain once more did nothing.

Later that year, Hitler demanded that Czechoslovakia give up land to Germany. Czechoslovakia refused. At the **Munich Conference** in September 1938, Germany, France, Britain, and Italy agreed to allow the Germans to take the land. In return, Hitler promised to respect the new borders of Czechoslovakia. A few months later, however, he took the entire country.

In the summer of 1939, Hitler made a similar demand of Poland. That nation also refused to give up land and turned to Britain and France for aid. But Hitler believed that Britain and France would not risk going to war. At the same time, he signed an agreement with Soviet dictator Joseph Stalin. The two countries promised never to attack one another.

The Axis Powers were moving unchecked at the end of the decade. The whole world was waiting to see what would happen next. Would it be war?

3. What happened at the Munich Conference?

_____

_____

Lesson 4, *continued*

As you read this lesson, take notes to answer the questions based on the timeline.

1931	**Japan invades Manchuria.**	1. Why did the Japanese invade Manchuria?
1935	**Mussolini invades Ethiopia.** **U.S. Congress passes first of three Neutrality Acts.**	2. Why did Britain and France take no action against Italian aggression?
		3. Why did isolationists want these laws passed?
1936	**German troops move into the Rhineland.**	4. What were some effects of appeasing Hitler after his invasion of the Rhineland?
1937	**Japan invades China.** **Hitler plans to absorb Austria and Czechoslovakia into the Third Reich.**	5. What were the immediate results of this invasion?
1938	**Munich Conference is held.**	6. Why was the Munich Conference unsuccessful?
1939	**Franco becomes Spanish dictator.** **Germany and Russia sign a nonaggression pact.**	7. Why did Stalin sign an agreement with fascist Germany, once a bitter enemy?

            Guided Reading Workbook

Hitler's Lightning War

Key Terms and People

nonaggression pact agreement in which nations promise not to attack one another

blitzkrieg warfare in which surprise air attacks are followed by massive attacks on land

Charles de Gaulle leader of the French government-in-exile

Winston Churchill leader of Great Britain

Battle of Britain a series of battles between British and German air forces fought over Britain in 1940–1941

Erwin Rommel German general who led troops in North Africa

Atlantic Charter declaration of principles issued by Winston Churchill and Franklin D. Roosevelt in August 1941

Before You Read

In the last lesson, you read about actions that led up to World War II.

In this lesson, you will learn about the first years of the war in Europe.

As You Read

Use a chart to record key information about early events of World War II in Europe and North Africa.

GERMANY SPARKS A NEW WAR IN EUROPE
What caused Britain and France to declare war?

In 1939, Adolf Hitler decided to move on Poland. He had already conquered Austria and Czechoslovakia. When Hitler signed a **nonaggression pact** with Joseph Stalin of the Soviet Union, they agreed not to attack each other. Secretly, they also agreed to split Poland between them.

So, on September 1, the German army invaded Poland in a surprise attack. Using planes, tanks, and troops, it moved suddenly in a technique called **blitzkrieg,** or "lightning war." Britain and France declared war, but Poland fell.

On September 17, after secret agreement with Hitler, Stalin invaded eastern Poland. Stalin then began annexing the regions covered in a second part of the agreement. Lithuania,

Lesson 1, continued

Latvia, and Estonia fell without a struggle. Finland fought back, but in March 1940, it was forced to surrender.

For seven months after Poland fell to the Germans, Europe was calm. France and Britain got their armies ready. They waited for Hitler's next move.

1. Why did Poland fall to the Germans so quickly?

_____

_____

THE FALL OF FRANCE; THE BATTLE OF BRITAIN
What happened when France and Britain were attacked?

Suddenly in April 1940, Hitler's armies invaded Denmark and Norway. Within two months, they also captured Belgium, the Netherlands, Luxembourg, and France. Part of the French army, led by **Charles de Gaulle,** escaped to Britain to continue the fight. By then, Italy had joined Germany in the war.

Great Britain—now led by **Winston Churchill**—stood alone. The German air force began bombing Britain. It wanted to weaken Britain before invading it. But the British air force fought back. It was helped by radar, a new electronic tracking system that warned of coming attacks. Also, the British had broken the German army's secret code. The **Battle of Britain** lasted many months. Unable to break British defenses, Hitler called off the attacks in May 1941.

2. Why did Germany fail to win the Battle of Britain?

_____

_____

THE MEDITERRANEAN AND THE EASTERN FRONT; THE UNITED STATES AIDS ITS ALLIES
How did the United States take sides?

Hitler then turned his attention to the east and to the Mediterranean. Germany sent troops under General **Erwin Rommel** to North Africa to help Italy fight the British. In April 1941, German armies quickly took control of Yugoslavia and Greece. In June, Hitler began a surprise invasion of the Soviet Union. The Germans quickly pushed deep into Soviet territory.

The Germans were stopped from taking Leningrad in the north. They then turned on Moscow, the Soviet capital. A strong Soviet counterattack, combined with fierce Russian winter weather, forced the Germans back. Moscow had been saved, and the battle had cost the Germans 500,000 lives.

President Roosevelt wanted to help the Allies. He asked Congress to allow Britain and France to buy American weapons. Soon, American ships were escorting British ships carrying guns bought from the United States. The U.S. ships had orders to fire on German submarines in the Atlantic.

Roosevelt met secretly with Churchill in August of 1941. Although the United States was not officially in the war, the two leaders issued a statement called the **Atlantic Charter.** It supported free trade and the right of people to form their own government.

3. Name two ways in which the United States supported the Allies.

_____

_____

As you read about war in Europe and North Africa, answer the
questions about the timeline.

1939		1. What did each leader gain from the secret agreement?
Aug.	**Hitler and Stalin sign a nonaggression pact.**	
Sept.	**Hitler invades Poland.**	2. What strategy did Hitler use to conquer Poland?
1940		3. What was Hitler's plan for conquering France?
April	**Hitler invades Denmark and Norway.**	
		4. What happend at Dunkirk?
June	**France surrenders.**	
Sept.	**German Luftwaffe begins bombing British cities.** **Italy moves to seize Egypt and the Suez Canal.**	5. What was the outcome of the Battle of Britain?
1941 **Feb.**	**Hitler sends Rommel to help Italian troops seize Egypt and the Suez Canal.**	6. What was the outcome of the fighting at Tobruk?
June	**Hitler invades the Soviet Union.**	7. How did Hitler's invasion compare with Napoleon's invasion of Russia?

World War II

Japan's Pacific Campaign

Key Terms and People

Isoroku Yamamoto Japanese admiral who decided that the U.S. fleet in Hawaii had to be destroyed

Pearl Harbor navy base in Hawaii attacked by the Japanese, Dec. 7, 1941

Battle of Midway 1942 sea and air battle in which American forces defeated Japanese forces near Midway Island in the Pacific

Douglas MacArthur U.S. general who commanded Allied forces in the Pacific

Battle of Guadalcanal six-month battle on the island of Guadalcanal in which American and Australian troops defeated Japanese defenders

Before You Read

In the last lesson, you read about the war against Hitler in Europe.

In this lesson, you will learn about the war against Japan in the Pacific.

As You Read

Use a chart to identify the outcomes and effects of major events of the war in the Pacific between 1941 and 1943.

SURPRISE ATTACK ON PEARL HARBOR

How did the United States fight Japan before declaring war?

The military leaders who ran the Japanese government also had plans to build an empire.

The Japanese captured part of China in 1931. In 1937, they invaded the center of China. There they met strong resistance. Needing resources for this war, they decided to move into Southeast Asia.

The United States feared that Japanese control of this area would threaten U.S. holdings in the Pacific. Roosevelt gave military aid to China. He also cut off oil shipments to Japan.

Japanese Admiral **Isoroku Yamamoto** decided that the U.S. fleet in Hawaii had to be destroyed. On December 7, 1941, the Japanese navy began a surprise attack on the U.S. naval base at **Pearl Harbor** in Hawaii. In just two hours, Japanese planes sank or damaged a major part of the U.S. Pacific fleet—19 ships, including 8 battleships. The next day, Congress, at the request of President Roosevelt, declared war on Japan and its allies.

1. How did the United States respond to the Japanese attack on Pearl Harbor?

_____

_____

JAPANESE VICTORIES
What areas of Asia did the Japanese conquer between December 1941 and mid-1942?

The Japanese attack on Pearl Harbor was just one of many sudden strikes. Japan also captured Guam, Wake Island, and the Philippines from the United States. It took Indonesia from the Dutch, and Hong Kong, Malaya, and Singapore from the British.

Japan then invaded Burma, located between India and China. Burma fell in May 1942. By that time, Japan had conquered more than 1 million square miles of land with about 150 million people.

Before these conquests, the Japanese had tried to win the support of Asians. They used the anticolonial slogan "Asia for the Asians." After their victory, the Japanese made it clear that they had come as conquerers.

While Japan often treated native people in their new colonies badly, they treated prisoners of war worse. On the Bataan Death March in the Philippines, thousands of prisoners under Japanese control died marching to a prison camp.

2. What countries lost territory to Japan early in the war?

_____

_____

THE ALLIES STRIKE BACK; AN ALLIED OFFENSIVE
How did the Allies strike back?

The Japanese seemed unbeatable after a string of victories. But the Allies wanted to strike back in the Pacific. In April 1942, the United States sent planes to drop bombs on Tokyo. The attack raised the morale of Americans. In May 1942, the Allies suffered heavy losses at the Battle of the Coral Sea. Still, they were able to stop the Japanese advance and save Australia.

The next month, the U.S. Navy scored an important victory near Midway Island in the central Pacific. In the **Battle of Midway,** Japan lost 332 planes and four aircraft carriers. The victory turned the tide of war against Japan.

The United States now went on the attack. General **Douglas MacArthur** did not want to invade the Japanese-held islands that were most strongly defended. He wanted to attack weaker ones and use these islands as bases for future attacks. The first attack came on Guadalcanal, in the Solomon Islands in August. The Japanese were building an air base there. It took six months of fighting for U.S. and Australian troops to drive the Japanese off the island in the **Battle of Guadalcanal.** The Japanese abandoned the island in February 1943.

3. Name three Allied victories against Japan.

_____

_____

Lesson 2, *continued*

As you read this lesson, answer the questions about the war in the Pacific.

a. What happened?
b. What is the significance of the battle or attack?

1. Bombing of Pearl Harbor	a. b.
2. Fall of Southeast Asian colonies	a. b.
3. Doolittle's raid on Japan	a. b.
4. Battle of the Coral Sea	a. b.
5. Battle of Midway	a. b.
6. Battle of Guadalcanal	a. b.

Guided Reading Workbook

World War II

Lesson 3

The Holocaust

Key Terms and People

Aryans to the Nazis, Germanic peoples who formed a "master race"

Holocaust systematic mass killing of Jews and other groups considered inferior by Nazis

Kristallnacht "Night of Broken Glass," when Nazis attacked Jews throughout Germany on November 9, 1939

ghettos neighborhoods in which European Jews were forced to live

"Final Solution" Hitler's plan to kill as many Jews as possible

genocide systematic killing of an entire people

Before You Read

In the last lesson, you read about World War II battles in the Pacific.

In this lesson, you will read about Hitler's "Final Solution" in Europe.

As You Read

Use a chart to organize ideas and details about the Holocaust.

THE HOLOCAUST BEGINS
What was the Holocaust?

Part of Hitler's new order for Europe included getting rid of "inferior" people. Hitler believed that the **Aryans,** or German peoples, were a "master race." He had a deep-seated hatred of people who were not German. He particularly hated Jews. This led to the **Holocaust,** the killing of millions of Jews and other civilians.

During the 1930s, Hitler passed laws that took away the rights of German Jews. One night in November 1938, Nazi mobs attacked Jews throughout Germany. They destroyed homes and businesses and killed or beat many

people. This night became known as *Kristallnacht,* or "Night of Broken Glass."

Kristallnacht was a major step-up in the Nazi policy of persecuting the Jews. The future for the Jews in Germany looked grim. Thousands of Jews tried to leave Germany. Other countries accepted a large number but were unwilling to take all those who wished to leave.

Hitler ordered all Jews in Germany and his conquered lands to live in certain parts of cities called **ghettos.** The Nazis then sealed off the ghettos with barbed wire and stone walls. They wanted the Jews inside to starve or die

Lesson 3, *continued*

of disease. Even under these horrible conditions, the Jews hung on.

1. How did the Holocaust begin?

_____

_____

THE "FINAL SOLUTION"
What was the Final Solution?

Hitler soon got tired of waiting for the Jews to starve or die of disease in the ghettos. He decided to take more direct action. He was going to kill as many Jews as possible.

Hitler's plan was the "**Final Solution**" to what the Nazis called the "Jewish problem." It was **genocide,** the systematic killing of an entire people. The Nazis also wanted to wipe out many other people to protect the "purity" of the Aryan race. These people included Roma (gypsies), Poles,

Russians, and those who were mentally or physically disabled. The Germans paid the most attention to Jews, however.

Thousands of Jews were shot to death by "killing squads." Millions were gathered and placed in concentration camps. These prisons used the inmates as slave workers. Many in the camps died of starvation or disease.

Starting in 1942, the Nazis built "death camps." At these camps, thousands of Jews were gassed to death in huge gas chambers. In the end, 6 million Jews were killed by the Nazis. Fewer than 4 million European Jews survived.

2. How was the Final Solution carried out?

_____

_____

Lesson 3, *continued*

As you read about the Holocaust, use the following questions to help summarize information in this section.

1. **Who?** Who were the victims of the Holocaust? Who were members of the "master race"?	
2. **What?** What were the Nuremberg Laws? What happened on the night of November 9, 1938? What was Hitler's "Final Solution"?	
3. **Where?** Where did German Jews try to migrate to find safety from Nazi terror? Where were Jews forced to live in German-controlled cities? Where were the concentration camps?	
4. **Why?** Why did Hitler believe that Jews and other "subhumans" had to be exterminated? Why did the Germans build extermination camps?	
5. **When?** When did the final stage of the Final Solution begin?	
6. **How?** How did non-Jewish people try to save Jews from the horrors of Nazism? How many Jews died in the Holocaust?	

The Allied Victory

Key Terms and People

Dwight D. Eisenhower American general who led the Allied invasions of North Africa and France (D-Day)

Battle of Stalingrad battle during which the Soviet Red Army forced the Germans out of Stalingrad

D-Day huge Allied invasion mounted to retake France from the Germans

Battle of the Bulge final large-scale attack by German troops that was forced back by the Allies

kamikaze Japanese suicide pilots trained to sink Allied ships

Before You Read

In the last lesson, you read about the Holocaust in Europe.

In this lesson, you will learn how the war was fought and brought to an end around the world.

As You Read

Use a chart to take notes on events that led to the Allies' victory in the war.

THE TIDE TURNS ON TWO FRONTS
Where **did the tide of war turn in favor of the Allies?**

In 1942, Roosevelt, Churchill, and Stalin planned the Allies' strategy. Stalin wanted Britain and the United States to open a second front against Germany to relieve the pressure on his armies. Stalin wanted the attack in France. Roosevelt and Churchill agreed to a second front but chose to attack German General Erwin Rommel in North Africa.

In late 1942, the British army led by General Bernard Montgomery drove the Germans out of Egypt and back to the west. Meanwhile, American troops under the command of General **Dwight D. Eisenhower** landed behind the

Germans and began moving east. The Germans were finally forced out of Africa in May 1943.

At the same time, the Soviets gained a major victory as well. German troops had invaded the Soviet city of Stalingrad in 1942. The Red Army forced the Germans to surrender in February 1943, ending the **Battle of Stalingrad.**

American and British soldiers next invaded Italy and captured Sicily in August 1943. Mussolini was driven from power, and the new Italian government surrendered. But Hitler did not want to give up Italy. His army fought there until 1945.

1. What major victories did the
   Allies win?

   _____

   _____

THE ALLIED HOME FRONTS
What problems did people face at home?

While the Allies continued to fight, people at home suffered. Many British and Soviet citizens died. In the United States, citizens faced shortages. Food, tires, gasoline, and clothing were in short supply. The government rationed, or limited, these items so there would be enough for the military.

Bitter feelings against the Japanese became widespread. As a result, mistrust of Japanese Americans grew. The U.S. government took thousands of Japanese Americans who lived on the West Coast and moved them to relocation camps in the western United States. Two-thirds of these people were American citizens.

2. What happened to Japanese
   Americans?

   _____

   _____

VICTORY IN EUROPE; VICTORY IN THE PACIFIC
What led to victory in the Pacific?

In early 1944, the Allies built a force to retake France. In June, an invasion of thousands of ships, planes, and soldiers was launched. It was called **D-Day.** The invasion force suffered heavy losses but gained a foothold in northern France. A month later, Allied forces began to pour through German lines. In August, they marched in triumph into Paris. Soon

after, they had driven the Germans out of France, Belgium, Luxembourg, and much of the Netherlands.

In late 1944, Hitler ordered one final, large-scale attack in the west. In the **Battle of the Bulge,** the German army punched through Allied lines until a counterattack forced it back. Meanwhile, the Soviets were pushing the Germans back in eastern Europe. By late April 1945, Soviet troops surrounded Berlin, Hitler's headquarters. During the Soviet shelling of Berlin, Hitler killed himself. A week later, the Germans surrendered. Roosevelt did not live to see this victory, however. He had died in early April. Harry Truman was now president.

In the Pacific, the Allies began to move toward Japan in 1943. They landed troops in the Philippines in the fall of 1944. In the Battle of Leyte Gulf, the Japanese navy was crushed.

As American troops moved closer to Japan, they faced attacks by **kamikaze.** These Japanese suicide pilots sank Allied ships by crashing their bomb-filled planes into them. In March 1945, U.S. Marines captured the island of Iwo Jima, a strategic Japanese stronghold. By June, they controlled Okinawa, an island just 350 miles from Japan.

The United States feared an invasion of Japan would cost too many Allied lives. In August, President Truman ordered an atomic bomb drop on the city of Hiroshima. A second bomb was dropped on Nagasaki three days later. Tens of thousands of Japanese died. Japan surrendered in September.

3. Name two events that led directly to
   Japan's surrender.

   _____

   _____

As you read this lesson, note how each of the following events or campaigns contributed to the Allies' victory in World War II.

1. Battle of El Alamein	2. Operation Torch
3. Battle of Stalingrad	4. Invasion of Italy
5. Propaganda campaigns on home fronts	6. D-Day invasion
7. Battle of the Bulge	8. Battle of Leyte Gulf
9. Battle of Okinawa	10. Bombing of Hiroshima and Nagasaki

World War II

Europe and Japan in Ruins

Key Terms and People

Nuremberg Trials trials of Nazi leaders charged with crimes against humanity, held in Nuremberg, Germany

demilitarization removing armed forces and weapons of a country

democratization process of creating a government elected by the people

Before You Read

In the last lesson, you read about how the war ended.

In this lesson, you will learn about the war's effects on Europe and Japan.

As You Read

Use a Venn diagram to compare and contrast conditions in postwar Europe and Japan.

DEVASTATION IN EUROPE
How did the war change Europe?

The war had left Europe in ruins. Almost 40 million people were dead. Hundreds of cities were reduced to rubble by constant bombing and shelling. The ground war had destroyed much of the countryside. Displaced persons from many nations were trying to get back home. Often there was no water, no electricity, and little food. Hunger was constant.

Agriculture had been disrupted. Most able-bodied men had served in the military, and the women had worked in war production. Few had remained to plant the fields. With factories destroyed or damaged, most people had no earnings to buy the food that was available. Also the small harvests did not reach the cities because the transportation system had been

destroyed. Suffering continued for many years in Europe.

1. What conditions existed in Europe after World War II?

_____

_____

POSTWAR GOVERNMENTS AND POLITICS
Who did the Europeans blame for the war?

Europeans often blamed their leaders for the war and its aftermath. Once Germany was defeated, some prewar governments—like those in Belgium, Holland, Denmark, and Norway—returned quickly. In Germany, Italy, and France, the old fascist governments had disappeared. At first, the Communist parties grew strong in France and Italy.

People who opposed Communism grew alarmed. They voted leaders from other parties into power. Communism lost its appeal when the economies of these lands improved.

During efforts to rebuild Europe, the Allies held the **Nuremberg Trials** in the German city of Nuremberg. There, captured Nazi leaders were charged with crimes against humanity. They were found guilty, and some were executed.

2. What were the Nuremberg Trials?

_____

_____

POSTWAR JAPAN; OCCUPATION BRINGS DEEP CHANGES
What changes were made in Japan?

The defeat suffered by Japan in World War II had devastated that country. Two million lives had been lost. The country's major cities were in ruins.

The U.S. Army occupied Japan under the command of General MacArthur. He began a process of **demilitarization,** removing the Japanese armed forces. MacArthur also paid attention to **democratization,** or creating a government elected by the people. His first step was to write a new constitution. It gave all power to the Japanese people, who voted for members of a parliament that would rule the land. All Japanese over age 20— including women—were given the right to vote. In 1951, other nations finally signed a formal peace with Japan. A few months later, U.S. military occupation ended.

3. How did the government of Japan change?

_____

_____

Guided Reading Workbook

Lesson 5, *continued*

As you read this lesson, fill out the chart by writing notes to describe conditions in postwar Europe and Japan.

Postwar Europe:	
1. Note three ways war affected the land and people of Europe.	
2. Note three political problems postwar governments faced.	
3. Note one way the Allies dealt with the Holocaust.	

Postwar Japan:	
4. Note two effects of Allied bombing raids on Japan.	
5. Note three ways U.S. occupation changed Japan.	
6. Note three provisions in Japan's new constitution.	

Cold War Conflicts

Cold War: Superpowers Face Off

Key Terms and People

United Nations world organization formed in 1945 to prevent war among nations

iron curtain division between Eastern and Western Europe during the Cold War

containment U.S. foreign policy aimed at preventing the spread of communism

Truman Doctrine policy of giving aid to countries threatened by communism

Marshall Plan U.S. plan to help European economies recover after World War II

Cold War state of tension and mistrust between the United States and the Soviet Union

NATO military alliance of the United States, Canada, and Western Europe

Warsaw Pact military alliance between the Soviet Union and Eastern Europe

brinkmanship policy of threatening to go to war in response to an enemy's aggression

Before You Read

In the last lesson, you learned about the war's effects on Europe and Japan.

In this lesson, you will learn about the international tensions that followed the war.

As You Read

Use a chart to record actions or policies that helped create the Cold War.

LONG-TERM CONSEQUENCES OF WORLD WAR II
What were some effects of World War II?

World War II was the most destructive war in history. Over 60 million soldiers and civilians died during the war. After the war, hunger and disease killed many others. The destruction of land and property and new national borders forced millions of people to move to new areas. Economies were ruined and some countries had to rebuild from almost nothing. Western European countries improved faster than countries under Soviet control.

1. What were some long-term consequences of World War II?

_____

_____

ALLIES BECOME ENEMIES; EASTERN EUROPE'S IRON CURTAIN

What caused the Cold War?

The United States and the Soviet Union were allies during World War II. In February 1945, they agreed to divide Germany into separate zones. The Allies also helped form the **United Nations** (UN). The UN pledged to prevent war.

After the war, there were striking differences between the United States and the Soviet Union. The United States suffered few casualties and was the richest nation in the world. The Soviet Union suffered enormous loss of life and damage to its cities. Politically, the United States wanted to encourage democracy. The Soviet Union wanted to set up Communist governments. These differences caused tensions.

At the end of World War II, the Soviets set up Communist governments in the occupied countries of Albania, Bulgaria, Hungary, Czechoslovakia, Romania, Poland, and Yugoslavia. This divided Europe between East and West. Winston Churchill called this division the "**iron curtain.**"

2. How did U.S. goals and Soviet goals differ after World War II?

_____

_____

UNITED STATES TRIES TO CONTAIN SOVIETS; THE COLD WAR DIVIDES THE WORLD

Why did tensions between the superpowers increase?

Truman began a policy of **containment**—blocking the Soviets from spreading communism. Under the **Truman Doctrine,** the United States helped nations that were threatened by communism. The United States also adopted the **Marshall Plan,** which gave food and other aid to European countries recovering from the war.

In 1948, the Soviets and Americans clashed over Germany. The Soviets cut off all transportation into Berlin, a divided city deep within the Soviet zone. The United States and Britain responded with the Berlin airlift. They flew supplies into the city for 11 months. Finally, the Soviets lifted the blockade.

The struggle between the United States and the Soviet Union was called the **Cold War.** Many countries supported one superpower or the other.

The United States, Canada, and several countries in Western Europe formed the North Atlantic Treaty Organization (**NATO**), a military alliance. The Soviets and Eastern European countries made a similar agreement called the **Warsaw Pact.**

By 1953, both superpowers had an even more deadly weapon than an atomic bomb—a hydrogen bomb. Each nation produced more and more nuclear weapons. Both sides were willing to go to the brink, or edge, of war. This became known as **brinkmanship.**

In 1957, the Soviet Union launched *Sputnik*, the world's first human-made satellite. The United States then began spending huge amounts of money to improve science education.

The U-2 incident brought more tension. The United States sent planes, called U-2 planes, to spy over Soviet territory. One was shot down in 1960.

3. What are three developments or events that increased tensions during the Cold War?

_____

_____

Lesson 1, *continued*

As you read this lesson, take notes to explain how each of the following actions or policies led to the Cold War between the United States and the Soviet Union.

1. Meeting at Potsdam, Germany	2. Policy of containment
3. Truman Doctrine	4. Marshall Plan
5. Blockade of Berlin	6. Formation of North Atlantic Treaty Organization (NATO)
7. Policy of brinkmanship	8. Launching of *Sputnik I*

Cold War Conflicts

Communists Take Power in China

Key Terms and People

Mao Zedong Communist leader who defeated the Nationalists and led the People's Republic of China

Jiang Jieshi Nationalist leader who set up a new government in Taiwan

commune large farms in China in which many families work the land and live together

Red Guards young Chinese students who carried out the Cultural Revolution

Cultural Revolution uprising in China between 1966 and 1976 that aimed to establish a society of peasants and workers in which all were equal

Before You Read

In the last lesson, you read about tensions between the superpowers.

In this lesson, you will read about civil war and the rise of communism in China.

As You Read

Use a chart to record information about the civil war in China and the creation of two Chinas.

COMMUNISTS VS. NATIONALISTS
Who fought the civil war?

Nationalists and Communists fought for control of China in the 1930s. During World War II, they joined forces to fight against the Japanese. The Communists, led by **Mao Zedong,** organized an army of peasants in northwestern China. From there they fought the Japanese in the northeast.

The Nationalists, led by **Jiang Jieshi,** controlled southwestern China. The Nationalists were protected from the Japanese by mountains. The United States sent the Nationalists large amounts of money and supplies, but corrupt officers took much of it. The Nationalists built a large army, but they only fought a few battles against the Japanese.

After the Japanese surrendered, the Communists and Nationalists resumed their civil war. The war lasted from 1946 to 1949. The Communists won because their troops were well trained in guerrilla warfare. They also enjoyed the backing of the peasants to whom they had promised land. In 1949, Jiang Jieshi and other Nationalist leaders fled to the island of Taiwan.

1. What two groups fought the civil war, and who led them?

_____

_____

THE TWO CHINAS AFFECT THE COLD WAR
How did the two Chinas participate in the Cold War?

. The United States helped the Nationalists set up a new government. The Nationalists called their land the Republic of China. Meanwhile, the Soviets helped Mao Zedong and his government, the People's Republic of China.

The Chinese and the Soviets promised to help defend each other if either country were attacked. The United States responded by trying to halt Soviet expansion in Asia. Communist China also tried to expand its power. The Chinese invaded Mongolia, Tibet, and India.

2. How did the superpowers take sides with the two Chinas?

_____

_____

THE COMMUNISTS TRANSFORM CHINA
How did Mao change China?

Mao set out to rebuild China. He seized land and gave it to the peasants. But he also forced the peasants—in groups of 200 to 300 households—to join collective farms, or **communes.** On these farms, the land belonged to the group. Mao also took control of China's industries. Under Mao's plan, production of industrial products went up.

With this success, Mao launched the Great Leap Forward. He wanted to make the communes larger and more productive. The plan failed. People did not like strong government control. The government did not plan effectively. Between 1958 and 1961, famine killed millions.

In 1966, Mao tried to revive the revolution. He encouraged young people to revive the revolution. Students formed groups called **Red Guards.** This was the beginning of the **Cultural Revolution.** The Red Guards struck at teachers, scientists, and artists. They shut down schools and sent intellectuals to the country to work on farms. They killed thousands of people who resisted. China was in chaos. Factories shut down and farm production dropped. Eventually, Mao put an end to the Cultural Revolution.

3. What are three changes Mao made?

_____

_____

As you read about the civil war in China and the creation of two
Chinas, take notes to answer the questions.

1. Who? Who was Mao Zedong? Who was Jiang Jieshi?	
2. When? When did the civil war in China resume? When did the civil war end?	
3. What? What advantages did Nationalist forces have? What advantages did Communist forces have?	
4. Where? Where is Nationalist China located? Where is the People's Republic of China located?	
5. How? How did the superpowers react to the existence of two Chinas? How did Mao transform the economy of China?	
6. Why? Why did the Great Leap Forward fail? Why did Mao launch the Cultural Revolution?	

Cold War Conflicts

Wars in Korea and Vietnam

Key Terms and People

38th parallel line that separated North Korea and South Korea

Douglas MacArthur leader of United Nations forces during the Korean War

Ho Chi Minh Vietnamese nationalist who drove the French out of Vietnam and who led North Vietnam

domino theory theory that nations were like a row of dominoes: if one fell to communism, the others would fall, too

Vietcong Communist rebels in South Vietnam who were supported by North Vietnam

Ngo Dinh Diem leader of the anti-Communist government of South Vietnam

Vietnamization Nixon's plan for gradually withdrawing U.S. troops from Vietnam and replacing them with South Vietnamese troops

Khmer Rouge Communist rebels who set up a brutal government in Cambodia

Before You Read

In the last lesson, you read about the civil war in China.

In this lesson, you will read about wars in Korea and Vietnam.

As You Read

Use a diagram to list causes and effects of the Korean and Vietnam wars.

WAR IN KOREA
How was Korea divided?

When World War II ended, Korea became a divided nation. North of the **38th parallel,** a line that crosses Korea at 38 degrees north latitude, the Japanese surrendered to the Soviets. South of that line, the Japanese surrendered to the allies.

As in Germany, two nations developed. The Soviet Union supported a Communist government in North Korea. The United States supported a non-Communist government in South Korea. On June 25, 1950, North Korea invaded South Korea, and captured almost all of South Korea. President Truman fought this aggression with help from the United Nations. The United States and other countries sent troops to assist South Korea.

This UN army made a bold counter attack. The attack was led by General **Douglas MacArthur.** In 1953, the two Koreas agreed to a cease-fire. The earlier boundary splitting North and South Korea remained the same.

North Korea had a Communist government. It had a large, strong army and tight government control, but it also had many economic problems. For more than 30 years, dictators ruled South Korea. But its economy grew, in part because it received U.S. aid. Free elections were held in South Korea after a new constitution was adopted in 1987.

1. How did the Korean War change the way Korea was divided?

_____

_____

WAR BREAKS OUT IN VIETNAM; THE UNITED STATES GETS INVOLVED; POSTWAR SOUTHEAST ASIA
How did the United States get involved in Vietnam?

A nationalist named **Ho Chi Minh** drove the French out of Vietnam in 1954. This worried the United States because Ho had turned to the Communists for help. Many Americans thought if one country became Communist, others would also, like a row of dominoes. This idea is known as the **domino theory.** A peace conference split Vietnam in two, with Ho taking charge of North Vietnam. The country had a Communist government. Communist rebels—the **Vietcong**— stayed active in the South.

The non-Communist government of the South had been set up by the United States and France. Its leader was **Ngo Dinh Diem.** When his government was threatened by Communists, the United States began to send troops. When they could not win the war on the ground, they tried bombing. Many people in the United States came to oppose the war.

In the late 1960s, President Richard Nixon began a plan called **Vietnamization.** This plan called for a gradual pullout of U.S. troops. At the same time, the South Vietnamese increased their combat role. The last American troops left in 1973. Two years later, North Vietnam overran the South and made Vietnam one country again. Today, Vietnam remains Communist but is looking for other nations to invest in its economy.

The fighting in Vietnam eventually spilled over into Vietnam's neighbor, Cambodia. Rebels there were known as the **Khmer Rouge.** In 1975, they set up a brutal Communist government. The Khmer Rouge killed 2 million people. In 1978, the Vietnamese invaded the country. They overthrew the Khmer Rouge. Vietnam withdrew in 1989. In 1993, Cambodia held free elections for the first time.

2. What happened in Vietnam after the United States withdrew?

_____

_____

As you read this lesson, fill out the chart below to help you better understand the causes and outcomes of wars in Asia.

War in Korea	
Causes	**Outcomes**
1. Why did the UN send an international force to Korea?	2. What was the legacy of the war for North Korea and South Korea?
French War in Vietnam	
Causes	**Outcomes**
3. Why did war break out between the Vietnamese nationalists and the French?	4. What was the outcome of the war for France and for Vietnam?
U.S. War in Vietnam	
Causes	**Outcomes**
5. How did the United States get involved in Vietnam?	6. Why did the United States withdraw its troops from Vietnam?

Cold War Conflicts

The Cold War Divides the World

Key Terms and People

Third World developing nations in Africa, Asia, and Latin America

nonaligned nations countries that did not take sides with either the United States or the Soviet Union

Fidel Castro Communist leader of Cuba

Anastasio Somoza Nicaraguan dictator

Daniel Ortega leader of Communist rebels in Nicaragua

Ayatollah Ruholla Khomeini Muslim leader who overthrew the shah of Iran

Before You Read

In the last lesson, you read about wars in Korea and Vietnam.

In this lesson, you will learn about Cold War struggles in other parts of the world.

As You Read

Use a chart to list main points about conflicts between the superpowers over Latin America and the Middle East.

FIGHTING FOR THE THIRD WORLD
How **were developing nations affected by the Cold War?**

After World War II, the world's nations were grouped into three "worlds." The First World included the United States and its allies. The Second World consisted of Communist nations led by the Soviet Union. The **Third World** was composed of developing nations in Africa, Asia, and Latin America.

Many Third World nations had serious problems. These problems were often due to a long history of colonialism. Some Third World nations faced political unrest that threatened the peace. Other problems included poverty and a lack of education and technology. Some of these countries tried to stay neutral in the Cold War. In 1954, they met to form what they called a "third force." It consisted of **nonaligned nations,** or countries that did not take sides between the Soviets and Americans. Others actively sought American or Soviet aid.

1. What problems did Third World nations face?

   _____

   _____

Lesson 4, *continued*

CONFRONTATIONS IN LATIN AMERICA
What happened in Latin America?

In Cuba in the 1950s, the United States supported a dictator. In 1959, a young lawyer, **Fidel Castro,** led a successful revolt. Castro received aid from the Soviet Union. In 1962, the Soviets and Americans almost went to war over nuclear missiles that the Soviets placed in Cuba. The Soviets finally pulled the missiles out. Over time, the Cuban economy became more dependent on Soviet aid. When the Soviet Union collapsed in 1991, this aid stopped. It was a serious blow to Cuba's economy.

The United States had also backed a dictator, **Anastasio Somoza,** in Nicaragua. Somoza's government fell to Communist rebels in 1979. The rebels were led by **Daniel Ortega.** When the new government began helping leftist rebels in nearby El Salvador, the United States struck back. It began to support Nicaraguan rebels that wanted to overthrow the Communists. The civil war in Nicaragua lasted more than a decade. Finally, the different sides agreed to hold free elections.

2. Where did Communists gain power in Latin America?

_____

_____

CONFRONTATIONS IN THE MIDDLE EAST
What happened in Iran and Afghanistan?

The Middle East often saw conflict between those who wanted a more modern, Western-style society and those who wanted to follow traditional Islam.

Such a struggle took place in Iran. In the 1950s, a group tried to take control of the government from Iran's ruler, Shah Mohammed Reza Pahlavi. The United States helped the shah defeat them.

Over time, the shah tried to weaken the influence of Islam in Iran. A Muslim leader, the **Ayatollah Ruholla Khomeini,** led a successful revolt. In 1979, the shah was forced to leave the country. Khomeini made Islamic law the law of the land. He followed a foreign policy that was strongly against the United States. He also led his country in a long war against its neighbor, Iraq.

The Soviets gained influence in Afghanistan after 1950. In the 1970s, Islamic rebels threatened the country's Communist government. The Soviets sent in troops to support the government. The United States felt its Middle East oil supplies were in danger and supported the rebels. In 1989, after a costly occupation, Soviet troops left Afghanistan.

3. How did Khomeini change Iran?

_____

_____

Guided Reading Workbook

As you read about conflict between the superpowers over Latin America and the Middle East, answer the questions about events listed in the timeline.

1959	**Fidel Castro leads a revolution in Cuba.**	1. How did revolution affect Cuba?
1961	**Castro turns back Cuban invasian at Bay of Pigs.**	2. Why did the United States support the invasion?
1962	**United States demands that Soviets withdraw missiles from Cuba.**	3. How was the Cuban missile crisis resolved?
		4. What were the consequences of civil war for Nicaragua?
1979	**Communist Sandinista rebels overthrow dictatorship in Nicaragua.**	
1981	**Iran releases U.S. hostages.**	5. Why did the Ayatollah Khomeini hate the United States?
		6. What part did the United States play in this Muslim war?
1988	**UN cease-fire ends hostilities between Iran and Iraq.**	
1989	**Soviet Union withdraws its forces from Afghanistan.**	7. How was the Soviet involvement in Afghanistan similar to U.S. involvement in Vietnam?

Cold War Conflicts

The Cold War Thaws

Key Terms and People

Nikita Khrushchev leader of the Soviet Union after Stalin, from 1953 to 1964

Leonid Brezhnev Soviet leader after Khrushchev, until 1982

John F. Kennedy president of the United States from 1961 to 1963

Lyndon Johnson president of the United States from 1963 to 1969

détente policy to decrease tensions between the superpowers

Richard M. Nixon president of the United States from 1969 to 1974

SALT talks to limit nuclear arms in the United States and the Soviet Union

Ronald Reagan president of the United States from 1981 to 1989

Margaret Thatcher prime minister of Great Britain from 1979 to 1990

Before You Read

In the last lesson, you read about Cold War struggles around the world.

In this lesson, you will read about the major events of the Cold War from the 1950s to the 1980s.

As You Read

Use an outline to organize main ideas and details about events in the continuing Cold War.

SOVIET POLICY IN EASTERN EUROPE AND CHINA
How did the Soviets keep control over Eastern Europe?

Nikita Khrushchev became the Soviet leader after Stalin died in 1953. Khrushchev began a process of "destalinization." This meant getting rid of Stalin's memory. Khrushchev also believed that the Soviet Union should have "peaceful competition" with the capitalist nations.

In Eastern Europe, many people still resented Soviet rule. Eastern Europeans took part in protest movements against

Soviet control. In 1956, protesters and the army overthrew the Communist government of Hungary. Khrushchev sent Soviet tanks to put the Communists back in power. In 1964, **Leonid Brezhnev** replaced Khrushchev. When Czechoslovakians began to reform their Communist government in 1968, Brezhnev sent in tanks to stop them.

The Soviets did not have the same control over their larger neighbor, China. Although the Soviet Union and China enjoyed friendly relations at first, they gradually grew apart. The split became so wide that the Soviet Union

Lesson 5, *continued*

and China sometimes fought along their border. The two nations now have a peaceful relationship.

1. In what two European countries did the Soviets put down revolts against Soviet control?

   _____

   _____

FROM BRINKMANSHIP TO DÉTENTE; THE COLLAPSE OF DÉTENTE

Did tensions between the United States and the Soviet Union change?

Tensions between the Soviets and the United States had been very high during the presidency of **John F. Kennedy.** They remained high during the presidency of **Lyndon Johnson.** The war in Vietnam helped keep relations tense.

In the early 1970s, the United States began to follow a policy called **détente** under President **Richard M. Nixon.** Détente was a policy of lowering tensions between the superpowers. Nixon made visits to both Communist China and the Soviet Union. In 1972, he and Brezhnev held meetings called the Strategic Arms Limitations Talks (**SALT**). They signed a treaty to limit the number of nuclear missiles each country could have.

The United States retreated from détente when the Soviet Union invaded Afghanistan in 1979. In 1981, **Ronald Reagan,** a fierce anti-Communist, became president. He proposed a costly antimissile defense system to protect America against Soviet missiles. It was never put into effect. But it remained a symbol of U.S. anti-Communist feelings. Like Reagan, British prime minister **Margaret Thatcher** was also strongly against Communism.

The Soviets grew angry over American support for the rebels fighting against the Communists in Nicaragua. Tensions between the United States and the Soviet Union increased until 1985 when a new leader came to power in the Soviet Union.

2. Name two actions or events that got in the way of détente.

   _____

   _____

Lesson 5, *continued*

As you read this lesson, take notes to answer the questions.

How did each country try to resist Soviet rule?		
1. Hungary	2. Czechoslovakia	3. China

What was the foreign policy of each U.S. president?			
4. John F. Kennedy	5. Lyndon Johnson	6. Richard Nixon	7. Ronald Reagan

What was the objective of each of the following?		
8. détente	9. SALT I Treaty	10. Strategic Defense Initiative (SDI)

The Colonies Become New Nations

The Indian Subcontinent Achieves Freedom

Key Terms and People

Rowlatt Acts laws to prevent Indians from protesting British actions

Amritsar Massacre a slaughter of Indians by the British at a peaceful protest in 1919

Mohandas K. Gandhi leader of the movement for Indian independence from Britain

civil disobedience disobeying the law for the purpose of achieving some higher goal

Salt March a march to the sea to protest British salt tax

Congress Party group consisting mostly of Hindus that led a campaign for India's independence

Muhammad Ali Jinnah leader of the Muslim League

Muslim League Muslim group that led a campaign for India's independence

partition division of India into two nations

Jawaharlal Nehru first prime minister of India

Indira Gandhi daughter of Nehru who followed him as prime minister

Benazir Bhutto former prime minister of Pakistan

Before You Read

In the last lesson you learned about the major events of the Cold War from the 1950s to the 1980s.

In this lesson, you will learn about nationalism in India and southwest Asia.

As You Read

Use a chart to list key points related to the independence of India, and new nations of Pakistan, Bangladesh, and Sri Lanka.

NATIONALISM SURFACES IN INDIA; GANDHI'S TACTICS OF NONVIOLENCE; BRITAIN GRANTS

LIMITED SELF-RULE; FREEDOM BRINGS TURMOIL; MODERN INDIA
What were Gandhi's ideas about nonviolence?

By the early 1900s, many Indians angry at British domination of Indian life were calling for self-government. After World War I, Britain promised to give more control of India to the Indian people. When they did not, Indians protested. The British Parliament then passed the **Rowlatt Acts,** which allowed protesters to be jailed without a trial.

Soon after, British troops killed several hundred peaceful protesters in Amritsar. After the **Amritsar Massacre,** millions of Indians changed from loyal British subjects to nationalists.

Mohandas K. Gandhi became the leader of India's protest movement. He had a deeply religious approach to political activity.

Gandhi organized a campaign of noncooperation with the British. It was based on passive resistance, or **civil disobedience,** to unjust laws. He asked Indians to take these actions without using violence.

Indians resented a British law that forced them to buy salt only from the government. Gandhi organized a huge protest called the **Salt March.** Soon afterward, Gandhi's independence movement gained worldwide support.

Two main political groups worked toward independence from Britain. The Indian National Congress, or the **Congress Party,** said that it represented all of India. Most of its members were Hindu. **Muhammad Ali Jinnah** formed the **Muslim League** in 1906. He said that the Congress Party did not care for the rights of Indian Muslims.

India gained independence in 1947, and created the separate Hindu and Muslim nations of India and Pakistan. This is called the **partition** of India.

Jawaharlal Nehru became the first prime minister of India. He tried to improve the status of the lower castes

and of women. In 1964, his daughter, **Indira Gandhi,** became prime minister. She took steps to increase food production. In 1984, she was killed by Sikh rebels. Separatist movements and tension between India and Pakistan continue to disrupt Indian society.

1. How did Indians use nonviolence to achieve their goals?

_____

_____

PAKISTAN COPES WITH FREEDOM; BANGLADESH AND SRI LANKA STRUGGLE
How have new political divisions led to violence?

When Pakistan was first formed, it had east and west parts separated by India. In a bloody fight in 1971, the eastern part won its independence, and became Bangladesh. Power struggles in Pakistan have continued. Its leaders have included Ali Bhutto and his daughter, **Benazir Bhutto.** She was elected prime minister twice. Nawaz Sharif is the current prime minister.

In 2011, U.S. forces killed Osama bin Laden in Pakistan. Pakistani officials had denied bin Laden was in Pakistan. This incident has increased distrust between the United States and Pakistan.

Ceylon, an island on the southeastern coast of India, won its independence in 1947 as well. In 1972, it was renamed Sri Lanka. In 2009, a Hindu minority on the island—the Tamils—lost a civil war to form a separate nation.

2. How was Bangladesh formed?

_____

_____

As you read about the independence of nations on the Indian subcontinent, take notes to answer questions about events listed in the timeline.

1940	Muslim League proposes partition of India at Lahore Conference.	1. What were the major concerns of the Muslim League?
1947	India and Pakistan become independent.	2. What problems had to be resolved in the months prior to independence?
1949	UN arranges cease-fire between India and Pakistan in Kashmir.	3. What were the terms of the cease-fire?
1964	Jawaharlal Nehru dies.	4. How did Nehru contribute to India's modernization and democracy?
1971	The nation of Bangladesh is formed.	5. What events led to the creation of this new nation?
1980	Indira Gandhi is reelected India's prime minister.	6. What major problem did Indira Gandhi face?
1987	Leaders of India and Sri Lanka reach an accord.	7. What was the cause of turmoil in Sri Lanka?

The Colonies Become New Nations

Southeast Asian Nations Gain Independence

Key Terms and People

Ferdinand Marcos leader of the Philippines who was elected but ruled as a dictator

Corazón Aquino woman who defeated Marcos in the elections of 1986

Aung San Suu Kyi daughter of Aung San; winner of Nobel Prize for her fight for democracy in Burma

Sukarno leader of Indonesian independence movement; first president of Indonesia

Suharto leader who turned Indonesia into a police state

Before You Read

In the last lesson, you read about independence and conflict in India.

In this lesson, you will read about independence and the challenges of self-rule in Southeast Asia.

As You Read

Use a chart to organize facts and details about Southeast Asian countries after independence.

THE PHILIPPINES ACHIEVES INDEPENDENCE
What happened in the Philippines after it gained independence?

In 1946, the United States gave the Philippines independence. The United States promised money to help the Filipinos rebuild their economy, however, the Filipinos had to agree to a trade deal. For the next few decades, the United States kept naval and air bases on the islands. Many Filipinos wanted the bases closed. In 1992, the United States left the bases.

From 1966 to 1986, **Ferdinand Marcos** led the country. He was elected president but after a few years ruled as a dictator. He then harshly put down dissent and stole millions of dollars from the country. When he lost an election to **Corazón Aquino** in 1986, he refused to leave office. A large public outcry forced him to step down. Aquino's son, Benigno S. Aquino III, later became president, in 2010.

For decades, Muslims known as Moros have tried to separate from the government. At times, the Moros have used violence to achieve their goals.

1. Who was Ferdinand Marcos?

_____

_____

2. What happened in Burma after it gained independence?

_____

_____

BRITISH COLONIES GAIN INDEPENDENCE
Which Southeast Asian British colonies won independence?

Burma was the first British colony in Southeast Asia to become independent. Nationalist leader Aung San helped drive the British out of Burma in 1948. Burma changed its name to Myanmar in 1989. Since 1962, generals have ruled the country. Myanmar has been torn by conflict often. **Aung San Suu Kyi** won the Nobel Peace Prize in 1991 for her opposition to this military rule. She has often been placed under arrest by the military government. But in 2012, she was elected to a government position. In the past few years, reforms have given the people of Myanmar more freedom.

After World War II, the British moved back into the Malay Peninsula. They tried to form a country there. But ethnic conflict between Malays and Chinese who lived in the area stopped them. In 1957, independence was given to Malaya, Singapore, and parts of two distant islands.

Singapore later declared independence as a city-state. Singapore is one of the busiest ports in the world. It is also a banking center. Its economy creates a high standard of living. Today, the government is trying to make health care, housing, and education cheaper for all of its citizens.

INDONESIA GAINS INDEPENDENCE FROM THE DUTCH
What challenges did Indonesia face?

Sukarno led an independence movement in Indonesia while Japan held that country. After World War II, he quickly declared an independent Indonesia. The Dutch at first tried to regain control over their former colony. But in 1949 they recognized Indonesia's independence.

Indonesia is spread out. It has 13,600 islands and includes people from 300 different groups that speak 250 different languages. It has been difficult for leaders to unite the nation. In 1967, a general named **Suharto** took control. He ruled until 1998. Many criticized him for taking over the island of East Timor and for corruption in his government. In the late 1990s Indonesia faced severe economic problems. Sukarno's daughter, Megawati Sukarnoputri, was president from 2001 to 2004. Since then, the large island country has made democratic reforms.

3. Why has governing Indonesia proven difficult?

_____

_____

Name _____ Class _____ Date _____

Lesson 2, *continued*

As you read about Southeast Asia, answer the questions that follow.

1. **What was the Bell Act?**	
a. Why did the Filipinos object to this act?	b. Why did they agree to sign it?

2. **Why did the United States demand a long lease on its military and naval bases in the Philippines?**

3. **Why does the Philippine constitution restrict the president to a single term of office?**

4. **What role did each play in recent Burmese history?**	
a. General Ne Win	b. National League for Democracy

5. **What is the current political status of these former British colonies?**		
a. Singapore	b. Malaya	c. Sarawak and Sabah

6. **What factors finally forced Indonesian dictator Suharto to step down?**

Guided Reading Workbook

The Colonies Become New Nations

New Nations in Africa

Key Terms and People

Negritude movement African movement after World War II to celebrate African culture, heritage, and values

Kwame Nkrumah leader in the Gold Coast independence movement

Jomo Kenyatta nationalist who helped lead Kenya to independence

Ahmed Ben Bella leader of the Algerian National Liberation Front who became the first president and prime minister of Algeria

Mobutu Sese Seko ruler who took control of the Congo in 1965 and renamed it Zaire

Before You Read

In the last lesson, you read about the struggle for self-rule in Southeast Asian colonies.

In this lesson, you will read about new nations in Africa.

As You Read

Use a chart to list problems and reforms that followed independence in Ghana, Kenya, Zaire, Algeria, and Angola.

ACHIEVING INDEPENDENCE
Why did independence movements increase after World War II?

During World War II, Africans fought as soldiers along with Europeans. After the war, Africans wanted independence. Many Africans took part in the **Negritude movement.** The purpose of this movement was to celebrate African culture, heritage, and values.

1. What was the Negritude movement?

_____

_____

GHANA LEADS THE WAY; FIGHTING FOR FREEDOM
What challenges did newly independent nations face?

The British gave Africans a greater part in the colonial government of its Gold Coast colony. **Kwame Nkrumah** led a movement to push Britain to act more quickly. The effort succeeded. In 1957, the Gold Coast colony became independent. The new nation took the name Ghana.

Nkrumah had big plans for building the economy of Ghana. But these plans were very expensive. Opposition grew. Finally, the army seized power in 1966. Since then, Ghana has shifted between

Lesson 3, *continued*

civilian and military rulers. There have been many economic problems. In 2000, there were open elections in Ghana for the first time, and these have continued.

The strong leadership of nationalist **Jomo Kenyatta** helped Kenya achieve independence in 1963. An uprising of Africans called Mau Mau also helped. Mau Mau aimed at frightening the British settlers to leave. Kenyatta became president of the new nation. He tried to unite the many different people in his country.

Ethnic conflicts and election disputes have often led to violence in Kenya. After a presidential election in 2007, more than 1,000 people were killed. In recent years, an Islamic militant group called al-Shababb has attacked Kenya.

There have been democratic reforms, however, in Kenya. The current president is Uhuru Kenyatta, Jomo Kenyatta's son.

A bloody conflict for independence took place in Algeria. About 1 million French settlers lived there. They were unwilling to give up their property or their control of the colonial government.

Violence broke out in 1945 and continued for many years. In 1954, the Algerian National Liberation Front, or FLN, announced its intention to fight for independence. In 1962, the French finally granted independence to Algeria.

Ahmed Ben Bella, a leader of the FLN, was the first prime minister and then the first president of Algeria. From 1965 until 1988, Algerians tried to modernize their country. These efforts failed.

An Islamic party won elections in 1991. But the government rejected the vote. Fighting between Islamic militants and the government continues in Algeria.

2. What problems did the new nations of Ghana and Kenya face?

_____

_____

CIVIL WAR IN CONGO AND ANGOLA
What happened in the Congo after independence?

The Congo won its independence from Belgium in 1960, but quickly fell into civil war.

In 1965, **Mobutu Sese Seko** took control. He renamed the country Zaire. Zaire had rich mineral resources. But Mobutu's harsh and corrupt rule made the country poor. He was overthrown in a coup in 1997. The country's name was changed back to the Congo. Since then, there have been elections and a new constitution, and even a peace agreement among rebel leaders. But ethnic fighting and corruption in the government also remain.

The colonies of Portugal were the last to gain their independence. After an independence movement broke out in Angola in the 1960s, Portugal sent in 50,000 troops. By the 1970s, the heavy cost of fighting had created opposition in Portugal to the war. The Portuguese left Angolia in 1975.

Angolans then fought a long civil war, which ended in 2002. The war left millions of people homeless and disease killed many others. Since the civil war, elected governments have worked to rebuild the country and keep the peace.

3. How did Mobutu rule the Congo?

_____

_____

Name _____ Class _____ Date _____

Lesson 3, *continued*

As you read this lesson, write notes about each African nation.
Describe how each nation gained independence and the reforms and
problems that followed independence.

1. **Ghana** Tactics used by Nkrumah:	Nkrumah's reforms:	Problems:

2. **Kenya** Tactics used by Mau Mau:	Kenyatta's reforms:	Problems:

3. **Zaire** How independence gained:	Mobutu's rule:	Problems:

4. **Algeria** How independence gained:	Ben Bella's program:	Problems:

5. **Angola** How independence gained:	Causes of civil war:	Other problems:

Guided Reading Workbook

The Colonies Become New Nations

Conflicts in the Middle East

Key Terms and People

Anwar Sadat Egyptian leader who signed a peace agreement with Israel

Golda Meir Israeli prime minister at the time of the 1973 Arab–Israeli war

PLO Palestinian Liberation Organization

Yasir Arafat leader of the PLO

Menachem Begin Israeli prime minister at the time of the Camp David Accords

Camp David Accords agreement in which Egypt recognized Israel as a nation and Israel gave the Sinai Peninsula back to Egypt

intifada sustained rebellion by the Palestinians

Oslo Peace Accords agreement aimed at giving Palestinians self-rule

Yitzhak Rabin Israeli prime minister at the time of the Oslo Peace Accords

Before You Read

In the last lesson, you read about conflicts in the new nations of Africa.

In this lesson, you will learn about conflict in the Middle East.

As You Read

Use a chart to list causes and effects of important political and military events related to Israel and its neighbors in the Middle East.

ISRAEL BECOMES A STATE
How did Israel come into being?

The movement to settle Jews in Palestine began in the late 1800s and early 1900s. These Jews believed that Palestine belonged to them because it was their home 3,000 years ago. But Muslims had lived there for the last 1,300 years.

After World War I, Britain took control of the area. The British found that Jews and Muslims did not live together peacefully. In 1917, Britain said it supported the establishment of a Jewish national homeland in Palestine.

After World War II, the British left the area. The United Nations divided the land into two parts. One part was set aside for the Palestinians, the other for Jews.

Islamic countries voted against the plan. The Palestinians opposed it. Many countries backed the idea of a separate Jewish state. They wanted to help make up for the suffering Jews had experienced in World War II. On May 14, 1948, the Jewish people in Palestine declared the existence of the Jewish state of Israel.

Lesson 4, *continued*

1. Why did the creation of Israel cause conflict?

_____

_____

2. What did the Suez Crisis and Six-Day War have in common?

_____

_____

ISRAEL AND THE ARAB STATES IN CONFLICT

How did Arab states respond to the creation of Israel?

On May 15, 1948, six Islamic nations invaded Israel. Israel won the war in a few months with strong support from the United States. This war was the first of many Arab–Israeli wars.

Another war was started by the Suez Crisis in 1956. Gamal Abdel Nasser, the new leader of Egypt, attacked the British-controlled Suez Canal. The Israeli army and French forces helped the British retake control. The peace settlement that followed gave the canal to Egypt anyway.

The Six-Day War broke out in 1967 when Egypt and other nations threatened Israel. Israel defeated Egypt, Iran, Jordan, and Syria in just a week. Israel's success brought new areas under its control.

The next war, in 1973, began when Egypt, led by **Anwar Sadat,** and its allies launched a surprise attack. At first, Arab forces won some of the territory lost in 1967. Israel, led by its prime minister, **Golda Meir,** fought back and won control of much of the territory it had lost.

The Palestinian Liberation Organization (**PLO**), led by **Yasir Arafat,** became the leading group in a struggle for an Arab Palestinian state on Israeli land. During the 1970s and 1980s, the military army of the PLO made many attacks on Israel.

EFFORTS AT PEACE; PEACE SLIPS AWAY

What happened at Camp David?

In 1977, Egyptian leader Sadat signed a peace agreement with Israeli Prime Minister **Menachem Begin.** Israel gave the Sinai Peninsula back to Egypt. In return, Egypt recognized Israel as a nation. This agreement, known as the **Camp David Accords,** was the first signed agreement between Israel and an Arab country. This angered many Arabs. Sadat was assassinated in 1981.

In 1982, Israel responded to PLO attacks by invading Lebanon to attack PLO bases there. In the late 1980s, many Palestinians in Israel began a revolt called the **intifada.** The intifada continued into the 1990s.

In the early 1990s, the two sides took steps toward peace. Israel agreed to give Palestinians control of an area called the Gaza Strip and of the town of Jericho. The agreement was known as the **Oslo Peace Accords.** The Israeli leader who signed this agreement, **Yitzhak Rabin,** was assassinated in 1995. He was killed by a Jewish extremist who opposed giving in to the Palestinians.

Since then, efforts have continued, but no peace deal between the Palestinians and Israelis has been reached.

3. What is significant about the Camp David Accords?

_____

_____

Lesson 4, *continued*

As you read this lesson, fill in the chart to describe cause-and-effect relationships in the Middle East.

Causes	Actions	Effects
	1. Britain promotes the idea of a Jewish homeland.	
	2. Independent Israel is created.	
	3. The 1956 Arab–Israeli war breaks out.	
	4. The 1967 Six-Day War begins.	
	5. The 1973 Yom Kippur War begins.	
	6. Sadat and Begin sign the Camp David Accords.	
	7. Rabin and Arafat issue a Declaration of Principles.	

Guided Reading Workbook

The Colonies Become New Nations

Lesson 5

Central Asia Struggles

Key Terms and People

Transcaucasian Republics the nations of Armenia, Azerbaijan, and Georgia

Central Asian Republics the nations of Uzbekistan, Turkmenistan, Tajikistan, Kazakhstan, and Kyrgyzstan

mujahideen a group that fought against the Soviet-supported government in Afghanistan

Taliban a conservative Islamic group that controlled most of Afghanistan from 1998 to 2001

Before You Read

In the last lesson, you read about conflicts in the Middle East.

In this lesson, you will learn how the nations of Central Asia have struggled to achieve freedom.

As You Read

Use an outline to organize main ideas and details about the challenges in Asian countries after the fall of the Soviet Union.

FREEDOM BRINGS NEW CHALLENGES
What **challenges have the countries of Central Asia faced?**

In 1991 the Soviet Union broke apart. As a result, the republics that it had conquered became fifteen independent states. These states include nine countries in Central Asia. One group of Central Asia states is known as the **Transcaucasian Republics.** The other group of states is called the **Central Asian Republics.**

Since independence, the countries of Central Asia have faced economic problems. These countries are some of the poorest in the world. They were helped economically by the Soviet Union. When they gained independence,

they had a hard time standing on their own. In addition, economic practices during the Soviet era created problems. For example, the Soviets made certain areas of Central Asia grow only one crop, such as cotton. Growing a single crop hurt the nations of Central Asia. They did not develop a balanced economy.

Central Asia is home to many different peoples. Some of these people have a history of hatred toward each other. When the Soviets ruled the region, they controlled these hatreds. However, after the Soviet Union broke apart, various groups began to fight. Some of these fights became regional wars, such as in Azerbaijan.

1. Why have countries in Central Asia faced economic problems?

_____

_____

AFGHANISTAN AND THE WORLD
How has Afghanistan struggled for freedom?

Afghanistan had a long history of struggle. During the 1800s, both Russia and Britain wanted to control Afghanistan. Britain fought three wars with the Afghanis. Eventually, Britain left the country in 1919.

In 1919, Afghanistan became an independent nation. It set up a monarchy, or rule by a king. In 1964, the country created a constitution. This constitution set up a more democratic style of government. However, the democratic system failed to grow.

In 1973, military leaders put an end to the democratic government. Five years later, a group took control of the country. This group was supported by the Soviet Union. Many Afghanis were against this group.

The Soviet-supported government had strong enemies. Many of these enemies formed a rebel group known as the **mujahideen,** or holy warriors. The mujahideen fought strongly against the Soviet-supported government. Then, Soviet troops invaded Afghanistan in 1979. The Soviets greatly outnumbered the rebels but could not defeat them. After 10 years of war, the Soviet troops left the country.

By 1998, an Islamic group known as the **Taliban** controlled most of Afghanistan. A rebel group, the Northern Alliance, held the northwest corner of the country.

The Taliban had an unusual understanding of the Islamic religion. Many other Muslims disagreed with this understanding. The Taliban believed that they should control nearly every part of Afghan life. Women were forbidden to go to school or hold jobs. The Taliban did not allow watching television or listening to modern music. Punishment for disobeying the rules included whipping and execution.

The Taliban allowed terrorist groups to train in Afghanistan. One group, al-Qaeda, was led by Osama bin Laden. Many believe this group has carried out attacks on the West, including the attacks on the World Trade Center. Those attacks happened in New York on September 11, 2001.

After the September 11 attacks, the U.S. government told the Taliban to turn over bin Laden. The Taliban refused. Then the United States took military action. In October 2001, U.S. forces began bombing Taliban air defense, airfields, and command centers. Al-Qaeda training camps were also bombed. On the ground, the United States helped the anti-Taliban Northern Alliance. By December, the United States had driven the Taliban from power.

The Afghanis then created a new government. Hamid Karzai was the leader of this government. Karzai, and now the current leaders of Afghanistan, have tried to rebuild the country. They also must deal with the Taliban, who remain in certain areas of the country.

2. What are some of the ways that the Taliban controlled Afghan society?

_____

_____

As you read about the struggles of Central Asia, take notes to answer
the following questions.

Freedom in Central Asia Brings New Challenges	
1. Since gaining independence, why have the nations of Central Asia struggled economically?	
2. Why have many regional wars been fought in Central Asia?	
Afghanistan Struggles for Freedom	
3. During the 1800s, why did Britain want to gain control over Afghanistan? Why did Russia want control over this region?	
4. Why did the Soviet Union invade Afghanistan in 1979?	
Rise and Fall of the Taliban	
5. How did rule by the Taliban affect Afghanistan?	
6. How did the United States help to defeat the Taliban?	

Struggles for Democracy

Democracy

Key Terms and People

Brasília capital city of Brazil

land reform breaking up large estates in order to give land to the landless

standard of living quality of life as judged by the amount of goods people have

recession decrease in the size of the economy

PRI Institutional Revolutionary Party, which has controlled Mexico for most of the last century

Before You Read

In the last lesson, you read about conflicts in the Middle East.

In this lesson, you will read about struggles for democracy in Latin America.

As You Read

Use a chart to take notes on democracy and the steps countries in Latin America have taken toward democracy.

DEMOCRACY AS A GOAL
How does democracy work?

For democracy to work, several conditions must exist. There must be free and fair elections involving more than one political party. The people should participate in public life. All citizens must accept the idea that the majority rules, but everyone has equal rights. Finally, there must be rule by law, not by power.

Many nations in Latin America have had difficulty achieving democracy because all these factors are not present.

1. Name four factors needed to make democracy work.

_____

_____

DICTATORS AND DEMOCRACY; STATE-SPONSORED TERROR
What challenges have Brazil and Chile faced?

After independence in 1822, Brazil was a monarchy. After 1930, a dictator ruled. But in 1956, Juscelino Kubitschek was elected president. He tried to improve the economy. He built a new capital city, **Brasília.** He supported **land reform.** Land reform aimed at breaking up large estates and giving land to the peasants.

Landowners opposed land reform. They backed army leaders who took power in 1964. The military ruled Brazil for 20 years. The country's economy grew. But the people had few rights. Eventually, their **standard of living** also fell. This means the quality of life, judged by the amount of goods people have, went down.

In the 1980s, a **recession** hurt Brazil. This economic slowdown was one factor in the return of democracy to Brazil. Since then, elections have been held in Brazil that have seen both probusiness and leftist candidates take office.

In 1970, leftist Salvador Allende was elected as president of Chile. Allende's Communist ideas threatened business interests in Chile and worried the U.S. government. The military took power in the early 1970s, and an army general, Augusto Pinochet, began a harsh political crackdown that involved murder and torture. Under international pressure, Pinochet agreed to reforms. After being charged for kidnapping and murder, Pinochet left office. Today, Chile is once again a democracy.

2. Why was Allende opposed in Chile?

_____

_____

ONE-PARTY RULE
What party has controlled Mexico for most of the century?

Mexico has had a stable government since the 1920s. One political party—now called the Institutional Revolutionary Party, or **PRI**—has been in power during most of this period, controlling local, state, and national governments. At times, the PRI acted harshly to stop any dissent. For example, in 1968 the government killed many people who took part in a demonstration for economic reform.

The PRI recently opened up the political system to candidates from other parties. In 1997, opposition parties won many seats in the national

legislature, ending PRI control of that congress. Then, in 2000, Mexican voters ended 71 years of PRI rule by electing Vicente Fox as president. In the years since, parties have competed in elections.

3. How has the PRI controlled Mexico?

_____

_____

POLITICAL AND ECONOMIC DISORDER; CHAOS IN CENTRAL AMERICA
How has democracy grown in Argentina and Guatemala?

Argentina has also struggled toward democracy. In the 1940s and 1950s, Juan Perón was a popular dictator. He put in place many programs to benefit the masses. But in 1955, the army overthrew him and controlled the government for many years. Army leaders ruled harshly. They killed many people who opposed them. In 1982, the army suffered a stinging defeat in a war with Britain. The generals agreed to step down. Since 1983, Argentina has been led by freely elected leaders.

In Guatemala, military dictators long controlled the government. Even after elections were held in the 1940s, the military stepped in and overthrew the government. The United States sided with the military, again fearing communism. A long civil war was fought. Although the civil war has official ended, Guatemala continues to struggle toward peace and democracy.

4. What happened after Perón was overthrown in Argentina?

_____

_____

As you read about democracy and democracy in Latin America, fill in the chart by writing notes in the appropriate spaces.

Making Democracy Work	
1. Note four practices that are common in a democracy.	
2. Note three conditions that contribute to democratic progress in a nation.	
Steps Toward Democracy in Latin America	
3. Note three actions Brazilian leaders took to stabilize Brazil's economy.	
4. Note one democratic practice in Brazil today.	
5. Note two steps involving Pinochet that helped lead to democracy in Chile.	
6. Note two crises that threatened democratic stability in Mexico.	
7. Note one way that the election of 2000 advanced democracy in Mexico.	
8. Note three ways military rule affected Argentina.	
9. Note one democratic practice in Argentina today.	
10. Note one reason the United States backed military rule in Guatemala.	

Struggles for Democracy

The Challenge of Democracy in Africa

Key Terms and People

federal system system in which power is shared between state governments and a central authority

martial law military rule

dissident person against government policy

apartheid strict separation of blacks and whites

Nelson Mandela leader of the African National Congress who was imprisoned

Before You Read

In the last lesson, you read about challenges to democracy in South America, Mexico, and Central America.

In this lesson, you will read about struggles for democracy in Africa.

As You Read

Use a chart to note the consequences of various policies and actions related to the struggle for democracy in Africa.

COLONIAL RULE LIMITS DEMOCRACY
What problems did colonial rule create?

African nations have had a hard time setting up democratic governments because of the effects of colonial rule. European powers made borders in Africa that paid no attention to ethnic groupings. They put people who disliked each other in the same area. This practice caused conflict.

Also, the European nations never built up the economies of their colonies. Most of the colonies lacked a middle class or skilled workers. Both are needed for a strong democracy. When Britain

and France gave their African colonies independence, they gave them democratic governments. But problems soon arose between rival groups.

1. Name three things that have slowed democracy in Africa.

_____

_____

CIVIL WAR IN NIGERIA; NIGERIA'S NATION-BUILDING
What happened after Nigeria gained independence?

In 1960, Nigeria became independent from Britain. It adopted a federal system. In a **federal system,** power is shared between state governments and a central authority. However, conflicts among the different peoples of Nigeria broke out. Army officers declared **martial law,** or military rule. The people of one ethnic group—the Igbo—tried to break away from Nigeria in 1967. The Igbo lost in a three-year civil war. Military rule continued.

In 1979, Nigeria got an elected government. Some army officers said the government was corrupt. The officers overthrew the government in 1983. The military rulers allowed elections in 1993. But they did not accept the results of the elections and continued to rule the land. They jailed **dissidents,** opponents of government policy. Only in 1999 was a civilian president elected. Presidents since have faced a variety of problems.

2. What happened after Nigeria's civil war?

_____

_____

SOUTH AFRICA UNDER APARTHEID
What was apartheid?

In South Africa, the conflict was between races. A white minority ruled a black majority. In 1948, the whites put in place a policy called **apartheid**—the strict separation of blacks and whites. Black South Africans were denied many basic rights. Some joined together in a group called the African National Congress (ANC) to fight for their rights. The white government cracked down on the ANC. They put many ANC leaders

in prison. **Nelson Mandela,** the leader of the ANC, was one of the people imprisoned.

3. Why was the African National Congress formed?

_____

_____

STRUGGLE FOR DEMOCRACY
How did apartheid end?

By the late 1980s, several riots had taken place. Blacks angrily struck back against apartheid. People in other nations also opposed apartheid. They refused to buy goods produced in South Africa. They hoped that isolating the country would persuade the South African government to end apartheid.

In 1990, President F. W. de Klerk took that step. He made the ANC legal and released ANC leader Nelson Mandela from prison. The South African parliament passed a law ending apartheid. In April 1994, all South Africans—even blacks—were able to vote in an election for a new leader. The ANC and Mandela won easily. In 1996, the new government approved a new constitution. It gave equal rights to all South Africans. Elections that have followed have seen peaceful transitions of power, although South Africa continues to face economic and social problems.

4. Why did F. W. de Klerk end apartheid?

_____

_____

As you read about Nigeria and South Africa, note the consequences of each of the policies or actions listed.

Policies/Actions	Consequences
1. In drawing up colonial boundaries in Africa, the colonial powers ignored ethnic and cultural divisions. →	
2. The colonial powers developed plantations and mines but few factories in Africa. →	
3. Civil war breaks out in ethnically divided Nigeria. →	
4. The military overthrows Nigeria's civilian government. →	
5. The National Party gains power in South Africa. →	
6. Riots break out in the black township of Soweto. →	
7. South Africans elect F.W. de Klerk president. →	
8. President de Klerk agrees to hold universal elections. →	

Struggles for Democracy

The Collapse of the Soviet Union

Key Terms and People

Politburo ruling committee of the Communist Party

Mikhail Gorbachev leader of the Soviet Union from 1985 to 1991

glasnost Gorbachev's policy of openness

perestroika Gorbachev's policy aimed at reforming the Soviet economy

Boris Yeltsin political opponent of Gorbachev who became president of Russia

CIS Commonwealth of Independent States, a loose federation of former Soviet territories

"shock therapy" Yeltsin's plan for changing the Soviet economy

Before You Read

In the last lesson, you read about political conflicts in Africa.

In this lesson, you will read about the fall of the Soviet Union and the rise of Russia.

As You Read

Use a chart to record important details about the collapse of the Soviet Union and developments in Russia.

GORBACHEV MOVES TOWARD DEMOCRACY; REFORMING THE ECONOMY AND POLITICS
How did Gorbachev open up Soviet society?

During the 1960s and 1970s, the leaders of the Soviet Union kept tight control on society. Leonid Brezhnev and the **Politburo**—the ruling committee of the Communist Party—crushed all political dissent. In 1985, Communist Party leaders named **Mikhail Gorbachev** as the leader of the Soviet Union. He was the youngest Soviet leader since Joseph Stalin. He was expected to make minor reforms. But his reforms led to a revolution.

Gorbachev felt that Soviet society could not improve without the free flow of ideas. He started a policy called **glasnost,** or openness. He opened churches. He let political prisoners out of prison. He allowed banned books to be published. Gorbachev also began a policy called **perestroika,** or economic restructuring. It tried to improve the Soviet economy by lifting the tight control on all managers and workers. In 1987, Gorbachev opened up the political system. He allowed the people to elect representatives to a legislature.

Finally, Gorbachev changed Soviet foreign policy. He moved to end the arms race against the United States.

1. What was the policy of perestroika?

_____

_____

THE SOVIET UNION FACES TURMOIL
What problems did the Soviet Union face?

People from many different ethnic groups in the Soviet Union began calling for the right to have their own nation. In 1990, Lithuania declared independence. Gorbachev sent troops. They fired on a crowd and killed 14 people. This action and the slow pace of reform cost Gorbachev support among the Soviet people.

Many people began to support **Boris Yeltsin.** At the same time, old-time Communists were becoming angry at Gorbachev. They thought his changes made the Soviet Union weaker. In August 1991, they tried to take control of the government. When the army refused to back the coup leaders, they gave up.

To strike back, the parliament voted to ban the party from any political activity. Meanwhile, more republics in the Soviet Union declared their independence. Russia and the 14 other republics each became independent states. Most of the republics then agreed to form the Commonwealth of Independent States, or **CIS,** a loose federation of former Soviet territories. By the end of 1991, the Soviet Union had ceased to exist.

2. Name three events that led up to the collapse of the Soviet Union.

_____

_____

RUSSIA UNDER BORIS YELTSIN
What happened when Gorbachev lost power?

After the coup failed, Gorbachev lost all power. Yeltsin became president. As leader of Russia, he faced many problems. He tried to change the economy. His economic plan was known as "**shock therapy.**" This move toward capitalism caused suffering.

In addition, rebels in the small republic of Chechnya declared their independence from Russia. Yeltsin refused to allow it. He sent thousands of troops to put down the Chechen rebels. As a bloody war raged, Yeltsin resigned and named Vladimir Putin as president.

3. What decisions did Yeltsin make about the economy?

_____

_____

RUSSIA UNDER VLADIMIR PUTIN
How did Putin handle the situation in Chechnya?

Putin dealt harshly with the rebellion in Chechnya, but then it dragged on for years. Chechen rebels seized a theater in Moscow, and more than 100 people died as a result.

Economic troubles continued as Russia dealt with social upheaval caused by years of change and reform. Social problems included homeless children, domestic violence, and unemployment, as well as declines in population, standard of living, and life expectancy.

4. What were some of the signs of social distress in Russia?

_____

_____

Lesson 3, *continued*

As you read this lesson, explain how Communist or Russian leaders responded to each problem or crisis.

Problems/Crises		Responses
1. Soviet society had stopped growing as a result of totalitarian policies banning political dissent.	→	
2. The Soviet economy was inefficient and unproductive.	→	
3. The Soviet–U.S. arms race had become too costly.	→	
4. In August 1991, hard-liners staged a coup against Gorbachev.	→	
5. The Soviet Union broke up.	→	
6. The Russian economy under Boris Yeltsin was ailing.	→	
7. In 1991, Chechnya declared its independence.	→	

Struggles for Democracy

Changes in Central and Eastern Europe

Key Terms and People

Solidarity Polish workers' movement

Lech Walesa leader of Solidarity

reunification uniting of East and West Germany into one nation

ethnic cleansing policy of murder and brutality aimed at ridding a country of a particular ethnic group

Before You Read

In the last lesson, you read about the collapse of the Soviet Union and the rise of Russia.

In this lesson, you will read about the fall of communism and other changes in Central and Eastern Europe.

As You Read

Use a chart to take notes to answer questions about changes in Central and Eastern Europe.

POLAND AND HUNGARY REFORM
How did Poland and Hungary change?

Gorbachev urged Communist leaders in Eastern Europe to change their policies, but many of them resisted. The people of Eastern Europe, however, wanted reform. Protest movements began to build.

In Poland, economic problems led Polish workers to organize a union called **Solidarity.** Solidarity went on strike to get the government's recognition. The government gave in to Solidarity's demands. Later, the government banned the union and jailed **Lech Walesa,** its leader. This caused unrest. Finally, the government was

forced to allow elections. The Polish people voted overwhelmingly for Solidarity. However, Poles became frustrated with the slow and painful road to economic recovery. In 1995, they voted Walesa out of office and replaced him as president first with a former Communist and then with more conservative leaders.

Inspired by the Poles, leaders in Hungary started a reform movement. The reformers took over the Communist Party. Then the party voted itself out of existence. In 1999, Hungary joined NATO as a full member. In recent years, conservative governments in Hungary have come under criticism.

1. What caused frustration and change in Poland?

_____

_____

GERMANY REUNIFIES
What changes occurred in Germany?

Thousands of people across East Germany demanded free elections. Soon, the Berlin Wall, which divided East and West Berlin, was torn down. By the end of 1989, the Communist Party was out of power. The next year, **reunification** occurred. The two parts of Germany, east and west, were one nation again. But the new nation had many problems. The biggest problem was the weak economy in the east. In time, however, the two parts of Germany have strengthened ties, and the German economy has grown.

2. What happened after the Berlin Wall fell?

_____

_____

DEMOCRACY SPREADS IN CZECHOSLOVAKIA; OVERTHROW IN ROMANIA
What happened in Czechoslovakia and Romania?

In Czechoslovakia, when the government cracked down on protesters, thousands of Czechs poured into the streets. One day, hundreds of thousands of people gathered in protest. The Communists agreed to give up power. Reformers launched an economic reform program that caused a sharp rise in unemployment that especially hurt Slovakia, the republic occupying the eastern third of the country. In 1993, the country split into two separate nations: the Czech Republic and Slovakia. The economies of both slowly improved.

In Romania, Nicolae Ceausescu, the Communist dictator, ordered the army to shoot at protesters. This caused larger protests. The army joined the people and fought Ceausescu. He was captured and executed in 1989. General elections quickly followed. Free-market economic reforms came more slowly.

3. How did the Communist rule end in Czechoslovakia and Romania?

_____

_____

THE BREAKUP OF YUGOSLAVIA
What happened in Yugoslavia?

Yugoslavia was made up of many different ethnic groups. In the early 1990s, they began fighting. When Serbia tried to control the government, two other republics—Slovenia and Croatia—declared independence. Slovenia beat back a Serbian invasion. But Serbia and Croatia fought a bloody war.

In 1992, Bosnia-Herzegovina also declared independence. Serbs in the region opposed the move. Using aid from Serbia, they fought a brutal civil war against the Bosnian Muslims. The Serbs used murder and brutality. This **ethnic cleansing** was intended to rid Bosnia of Muslims. The United Nations helped create a peace agreement.

In 1998, the area experienced violence again in Kosovo, a province in southern Serbia, which Serbian forces invaded in order to suppress an independence movement. A NATO bombing campaign forced Serbians to withdraw.

4. Who fought in the civil war in Yugoslavia?

_____

_____

Lesson 4, *continued*

As you read about changes in Central and Eastern Europe, take notes
to answer the questions.

Poland and Hungary Reform	
1. Why did the Poles choose a former Communist leader over Lech Walesa in the 1995 election?	
2. What were some of the reforms introduced in Hungary?	
Germany Reunifies	
3. Why did huge demonstrations break out throughout East Germany?	
Democracy Spreads in Czechoslovakia	
4. Why did Czechoslovakia break up?	
Overthrow in Romania	
5. What brought about Ceausescu's downfall in Romania?	
The Breakup of Yugoslavia	
6. What happened after Bosnia-Herzegovina declared independence?	

Struggles for Democracy

China: Reform and Reaction

Key Terms and People

Zhou Enlai Chinese leader who worked with President Nixon to improve U.S.–Chinese relations

Deng Xiaoping Chinese leader after Zhou Enlai

Four Modernizations goals of Deng Xiaoping that called for progress in agriculture, industry, defense, and science and technology

Tiananmen Square square in the capital of Beijing; scene of a student demonstration and massacre

Hong Kong island that became part of China again in 1997

Before You Read

In the last lesson, you read about the collapse of communism and other changes in Central and Eastern Europe.

In this lesson, you will learn about the recent history of China.

As You Read

Use a chart to note the goals and outcomes of actions taken in Communist China.

THE LEGACY OF MAO
How did Mao change China?

Mao Zedong's policies to build China failed to create a strong economy. Actually, they reduced incentives for higher production. One plan, called the Great Leap Forward, helped cause an economic disaster. Another policy of Mao's, the Cultural Revolution, caused social and political chaos. **Zhou Enlai,** another Chinese leader, worked to restrain radical policies.

1. How successful were Mao's economic programs?

_____

_____

CHINA AND THE WEST
How did Deng Xiaoping change China?

During Mao's rule, China had little role in world affairs. Zhou worried about this. He worked with U.S. President Richard Nixon to improve U.S.–Chinese relations.

After Mao and Zhou died in 1976, moderates took control of the government. The most powerful leader was **Deng Xiaoping.** He tried to modernize the economy. Deng had goals known as the **Four Modernizations.** These called for progress in agriculture, industry, defense, and science and technology. He ended farming communes and allowed farmers to sell

Lesson 5, *continued*

part of their produce for a profit. Farm production increased greatly.

Deng made similar changes to industry. People's incomes began to rise. They began to purchase appliances and other goods that were once scarce.

2. What were the results of Deng Xiaoping's changes?

_____

_____

MASSACRE IN TIANANMEN SQUARE

What caused the protest at Tiananmen Square?

Deng's new plan caused problems. The gap between rich and poor grew wider, which caused unrest. Western political ideas spread throughout the country. In 1989, thousands of Chinese students gathered in **Tiananmen Square** in the capital of Beijing. They called for democracy and freedom. Deng responded by sending army troops and tanks to put down the rally. Thousands were killed or wounded. China has continued to stamp out protests since then.

3. What happened to the protesters at Tiananmen Square?

_____

_____

CHINA ENTERS THE NEW MILLENNIUM

What happened to Hong Kong?

Deng died in 1997. He was succeeded as leader first by Jiang Zemin and then by Hu Jintao. Both leaders have continued economic reforms while keeping the government's strict control over society.

A major issue for China during this time was the status of **Hong Kong.** The island became part of China again in 1997 when the British gave it back after 155 years of colonial rule. China promised to respect Hong Kong's freedom for 50 years. But many worried that China would take away Hong Kong's freedoms.

4. Why do people worry about Hong Kong's new rule?

_____

_____

CHINA BEYOND 2000

What is the connection between political and economic reform in China?

Liberal economic reforms in China have not immediately led to political reforms. China has been successful in reducing poverty, in part because it has been cautious in privatizing the economy. China managed to maintain economic growth in the early 21st century. However, the gap between rural and urban areas has widened. The growth of industry has also caused environmental issues.

Some people in the West hope stronger relations with China will lead to political change. An important sign of China's engagement with the world was its successful campaign to be chosen as the site for the 2008 Summer Olympics.

5. Which has came first in China— political or economic reform?

_____

_____

As you read about Communist China, fill in the chart by noting the
goals and outcomes of each action listed.

Goals	Actions	Outcomes
	1. Mao begins the Cultural Revolution.	
	2. Zhou Enlai invites the American table tennis team to tour China.	
	3. Deng Xiaoping launches a bold program of economic reforms.	
	4. Students stage an uprising in Tiananmen Square.	
	5. Britain hands Hong Kong over to China.	

Global Interdependence

Science and Technology Transform Life

Key Terms and People

International Space Station project involving 16 nations to build a huge laboratory in space

Internet worldwide computer network

genetic engineering use of genes to develop new products and cures

cloning process of creating identical copies of DNA for research and other purposes

green revolution attempt to increase food resources worldwide

Before You Read

In the last lesson, you read about struggles for democracy in China.

In this lesson, you will learn about recent changes in science and technology.

As You Read

Use a chart to list the effects of scientific and technological developments in different areas.

EXPLORING THE SOLAR SYSTEM AND BEYOND
How did competition give way to cooperation in space?

From the 1950s to the 1970s, the United States and Soviet Union took their Cold War rivalry to space. Each nation tried to be the first to reach the moon and beyond.

In the 1970s, the two nations began to cooperate in space exploration. In 1975, United States and Soviet spacecraft docked, or joined together, in space. Later, American and Soviet space missions included scientists from other countries. In the late 1990s, the United States, Russia, and 14 other nations began working together to build the **International Space Station.**

Some space missions did not include human crew members. Unmanned flights sent back pictures and information about other planets.

In 1990, the United States and European countries sent the Hubble Space Telescope into orbit around the earth. This satellite still sends back unique images of objects in space. In recent years, the United States has landed robotic rovers on Mars.

1. Give three examples of international cooperation in space.

_____

_____

EXPANDING GLOBAL COMMUNICATIONS
How has technology changed communications?

Every day, satellites are used to connect people on a global scale. Satellites, for instance, allow television broadcasts to carry events live around the world.

Another huge advance in technology has been the computer. Computers have become more powerful since they were first invented. At the same time, they have gotten smaller in size. Consumer goods, such as microwave ovens, smartphones, and cars, often include computers and silicon chips to keep them running.

Millions of people around the world use personal computers at work or at home. Many of these people are connected through the Internet, a worldwide computer network. The **Internet** allows people to get a great deal of information more quickly and easily than ever before. It also allows people to communicate ideas and exchange cultural values from different parts of the world. The Internet and computers have changed how many people work and live.

2. How have computers changed everyday living?

_____

_____

TRANSFORMING HUMAN LIFE
How has new technology changed medicine?

New technology has changed medicine. Lasers allow doctors to perform surgery to fix problems in delicate areas, such as in the eye or the brain. New methods for making images of the body help doctors locate problems.

Research into genes has helped unlock the secrets of some diseases. **Genetic engineering** enables scientists to use genes in new ways. For example, scientists can develop plants with special traits. **Cloning** is the creation of identical copies of DNA. It is part of genetic engineering. Cloning can be used to produce plants and animals that are identical to existing plants and animals. The application of this new understanding of genes has led to many developments in agriculture.

Scientists have made other advances in farming. In the **green revolution,** scientists have developed new strains of food crops to help farmers grow more food. Although there are some risks in changing gene structures in plants, the goal is to increase food production worldwide.

3. Why is genetic engineering an important development?

_____

_____

Lesson 1, *continued*

As you read, fill out the chart by listing examples of technological progress in each of the following areas.

1. **Space exploration**	2. **Astronomy**	3. **Communications**
4. **Health and medicine**	5. **Genetics**	6. **Agriculture**

Guided Reading Workbook

Global Interdependence

Global Economic Development

Key Terms and People

developed nation industrialized nation with advanced manufacturing production

emerging nation nation that is still developing industry

gross domestic product GDP; a measure of the health of a country's economy

global economy economy linking the economies of many nations

globalization spread of economic and cultural influences around the world

free trade absence of barriers that can block trade between countries

ozone layer layer of atmosphere that blocks dangerous rays from the sun

sustainable development economic growth that meets current needs but conserves resources for the future

Before You Read

In the last lesson, you read about changes in science and technology.

In this lesson, you will read about the new global economy.

As You Read

Use a chart to identify causes and effects of forces that have shaped the global economy.

ECONOMIC OPPORTUNITIES AND CHALLENGES
How have the economies of the developed nations changed?

Technology has changed the world's economies. In the 1950s, scientists found new ways to make plastics, which came to be widely used. In recent years, industries have begun using robots to make products. These changes have required workers to have more and different skills than before.

In industrialized nations, or **developed nations,** there are more jobs in service and information industries. In the emerging nations, where wages are lower, manufacturing jobs began to grow more quickly.

Gross domestic product (GDP) is a way to measure the strength of an economy. Developed nations have the highest GDPs. These nations are mostly in Europe, North America, and parts of Asia. The least developed nations are mostly in Africa and southern Asia. Countries in these regions have low GDPs because they have poor education systems, weak political systems, and high levels of poverty. There may also be wars or other conflicts in these regions.

It is hard for these countries to compete in the global economy.

1. What types of jobs are on the increase in developed nations?

_____

_____

ECONOMIC GLOBALIZATION; IMPACT OF GLOBAL DEVELOPMENT

How **has the development of the global economy affected the use of energy and other resources?**

In recent decades, a **global economy** has been growing faster than ever before. Telephone and computer links connect banks and other financial companies around the world. Multinational corporations operate in many countries. **Globalization** is the spreading of economic and cultural influences. It results from an increasing global economy.

After World War II, many leaders believed that world economies would grow best if there was **free trade.** This means there would be no barriers to block goods from one country entering another country. In 1951, some nations in Europe joined together to create free trade. That group, now called the European Union (EU), has grown to become a powerful trading bloc.

The United States, Canada, and Mexico adopted the North American Free Trade Agreement (NAFTA) in 1994. Other free trade zones have been set up in Asia, Africa, Latin America, and the South Pacific.

In recent years, there has been considerable disagreement on the impact of the globalization of the economy. Supporters suggest that open, competitive markets and the free flow of goods, services, technology, and investments benefit all nations. Opponents charge that globalization has been a disaster for the poorest countries. Many, they suggest, are worse off today than they were in the past.

In 2007, an economic crisis struck rich and poor nations around the world. Financial and economic problems spread throughout the global economy. Many countries are still trying to recover from this crisis.

Economic growth needs many resources. Manufacturing and trade both use huge amounts of energy. Oil has been a major source of this energy. Whenever the flow of oil has been threatened, the world's economies have suffered shocks.

In 1990, Iraq invaded Kuwait. This threatened the flow of Kuwaiti oil. Soon, the countries of the United Nations went to war against Iraq. This was known as the Gulf War.

Economic growth has also caused environmental problems. Burning coal and oil has polluted the air. It has also caused acid rain and contributed to global warming. The release of some chemicals into the air has weakened Earth's **ozone layer.** This layer of atmosphere blocks dangerous rays from the sun.

One new idea about growth involves **sustainable development.** Sustainable development means keeping economies growing while conserving future resources.

2. What environmental problems have resulted from economic growth?

_____

_____

Lesson 2, *continued*

As you read about global economics, complete the chart by filling in
the cause or effect.

Causes	Effects
1.	Manufacturing jobs moved out of developed nations to emerging nations.
2. Multinational companies developed worldwide; computer linkages made business transactions easier and faster.	
3.	The United States, Canada, and Mexico signed NAFTA.
4. Activities essential for industry and trade require the use of much energy.	
5. Manufacturing processes release chemicals called chlorofluorocarbons.	
6.	Many plants and animals are becoming extinct.

Global Interdependence

Global Security Issues

Key Terms and People

refugees people who leave their country and move to another to find safety

supranational union alliance to increase security through political and economic unity

proliferation spread

Universal Declaration of Human Rights 1948 United Nations statement of specific rights that all people should have

nonbinding agreement agreement without penalty for not meeting the terms of it

political dissent difference of opinion over political issues

gender inequality difference between men and women in terms of wealth and status

AIDS acquired immune deficiency syndrome, a disease that attacks the immune system, leaving sufferers open to deadly infections

Before You Read

In the last lesson, you read about the growth of the global economy.

In this lesson, you will read about challenges to global security.

As You Read

Use a chart to list methods employed to increase global security and issues that threaten it.

ISSUES OF WAR AND PEACE
How have nations worked together for global security?

After World War II, nations joined together to pursue global security. The United Nations (UN) was formed at the end of World War II to promote world peace. The UN provides a place for countries—or groups within countries—to share their views.

The UN can also send troops as a peacekeeping force. These soldiers—who come from member nations—try to stop violence from breaking out. The UN also helps to move **refugees**—people moving from one country to another seeking safety.

The European Union is an example of a **supranational union.** The EU is an alliance to increase security through political and economic unity.

Another approach to world peace has been to limit weapons of mass destruction. These include nuclear weapons, chemical weapons, and biological weapons. In 1968, many nations signed a Nuclear Non-Proliferation Treaty. The nations that signed the treaty agreed to prevent the **proliferation,** or spread, of nuclear weapons. In the 1980s, the United States and Russia talked about destroying some nuclear weapons. In another treaty, many nations promised not to develop chemical or biological weapons.

Ethnic and religious differences are the sources of many world conflicts. Governments and many international organizations, including the UN, try to find peaceful solutions to such conflicts.

1. Name two specific approaches toward collective security.

_____

_____

HUMAN RIGHTS ISSUES; COMBATTING HUMAN RIGHTS ISSUES; HEALTH ISSUES; POPULATION MOVEMENT

What are some of the causes of the global movement of people?

In 1948, the UN approved the **Universal Declaration of Human Rights.** This declaration gives a list of rights that all people should have. In 1975, many nations signed the Helsinki Accords, which also support human rights. These are examples of **nonbinding agreements.** There is no penalty for not meeting the terms of the agreement. Many groups around the world, however, watch to see how well nations do in protecting these rights for their people.

One type of human rights violation occurs when governments try to stamp out **political dissent.** In many countries, individuals and groups have been persecuted for holding political views that differ from those of the government.

In the past, women suffered considerable discrimination. However, a heightened awareness of human rights encouraged women to work to improve their lives. They pushed for new laws that gave them greater equality. Since the 1970s, women have made notable gains, especially in the areas of education and work. Even so, **gender inequality** still is an issue.

Recently, the enjoyment of a decent standard of health has become recognized as a basic human right. However, for many people across the world, poor health is still the norm. Perhaps the greatest global challenge to the attainment of good health is **AIDS,** or acquired immune deficiency syndrome. AIDS is a worldwide problem. However, sub-Saharan Africa has suffered most from the epidemic.

In recent years, millions of people have moved from one country to another. Some people are refugees. Others leave for more positive reasons— the chance of a better life for themselves and their children.

While people have a right to leave, every country does not have to accept them. Sometimes these people have to live in crowded refugee camps. They suffer hunger and disease. They can also cause political problems for the country where they are held. However, immigrants also can bring many benefits to their new home.

2. What problems can result from the global movement of people?

_____

_____

As you read, fill out the chart by writing answers about global security in the appropriate boxes.

How do the following help to ensure collective security?	
1. Military alliances	
2. United Nations	
3. Nuclear Non-Proliferation Treaty	

How have the following threatened global security?	
4. Ethnic and religious rivalries	
5. Health issues	

How have the following promoted the cause of human rights?	
6. Universal Declaration of Human Rights	
7. Women's rights movement	
8. Migration	

Global Interdependence

Terrorism

Key Terms and People

terrorism use of violence against people or property to force changes in societies or governments

cyberterrorism attacks on information systems for political reasons

Department of Homeland Security department of the U.S. government that organizes the fight against terrorism in the United States

USA PATRIOT Act antiterrorism law that allows the government certain rights to help chase and capture terrorists

---

Before You Read

In the last lesson, you read about global security issues.

In this lesson, you will learn about terrorism and its effect on today's world.

As You Read

Use a chart to take notes about September 11 and other terrorist attacks, and policies to prevent future attacks.

WHAT IS TERRORISM?; TERRORISM AROUND THE WORLD
What motivates terrorists, and what methods do they use?

Terrorism is the use of violence against people or property to force changes in societies or governments. The reasons for modern terrorism are many. Reasons include gaining independence, getting rid of foreigners, and changing society. In the late 20th century, another type of terrorist appeared. These terrorists wanted to destroy what they believed were the forces of evil.

Terrorists use violence to try to achieve their goals. Terrorists often use bombs and bullets. Some terrorist groups have used biological and

chemical weapons. Attacks on information systems such as computer networks are called **cyberterrorism.** These attacks are done for political reasons. To fight terrorism, governments use many different strategies.

In the Middle East, Palestinians and Israelis have argued for decades about land ownership. This argument has resulted in many terrorist acts. In Northern Ireland, the Irish Republican Army (IRA) carried out terrorist acts for many years. The IRA wanted the British to give up control over Northern Ireland. Peace was reached in 2005.

Many terrorist groups, such as Aum Shinrikyo and the Tamil Tigers, are found in Asia. In Africa, civil unrest and

Lesson 4, *continued*

regional wars cause most terrorist acts. Narcoterrorism often happens in Latin America. Narcoterrorism is terrorism that is connected with the trade of illegal drugs.

1. What types of weapons do terrorists use?

_____

_____

ATTACK ON THE UNITED STATES; THE UNITED STATES RESPONDS; GLOBAL EFFECTS OF TERRORISM
How has the United States fought back against terrorism?

On the morning of September 11, 2001, Arab terrorists hijacked four airliners. The hijackers crashed two of the jets into the twin towers of the World Trade Center in New York City. The third jet destroyed part of the Pentagon in Washington, DC. The fourth plane crashed in an empty field in Pennsylvania.

The twin towers fell to the ground within two hours. About 3,000 people died in all the attacks. The dead included more than 340 New York City firefighters and 60 police officers.

Before September 11, many Americans believed terrorism was something that happened elsewhere. After September 11, many Americans became afraid that terrorist attacks could happen to them.

After September 11, the United States asked for an international effort to fight terrorism. U.S. officials suspected that Osama bin Laden had directed the September 11 attacks. Bin Laden was the leader of a terrorist group called al-Qaeda. In 2011, he was killed in Pakistan by U.S. Navy commandos.

The U.S. government created the **Department of Homeland Security** in 2002. Its job was to organize the fight against terrorism in the United States.

U.S. officials began to search for al-Qaeda terrorists. In addition, U.S. officials arrested and questioned many Arabs and other Muslims. Critics said that arresting people because of nationality or religion was unfair.

The **USA PATRIOT Act** became law. This law allowed the government several powers to help capture terrorists.

The Federal Aviation Administration (FAA) ordered airlines to put bars on cockpit doors to help stop hijackers. National Guard troops began to guard airports. Trained security officers called sky marshals were put on planes. The Aviation and Transportation Security Act was passed. It put the federal government in charge of airport security.

Since the 9/11 attacks in the United States, there have been many other terrorist attacks around the world. New technology and shared information have helped different countries work together to stop terrorism. Military agreements between countries have helped kill terrorists.

Terrorism affects many parts of society. It creates fear and insecurity in the population. It can cause instability in financial markets and stop tourism. There are also the costs of added security and military spending to fight terrorism. Governments must balance these costs with other needs.

2. How do the Department of Homeland Security and USA PATRIOT Act help fight terrorism?

_____

_____

Lesson 4, *continued*

As you read about terrorism, take notes to answer the questions.

1. **Who?** Who was Osama bin Laden? Who are sky marshals?	
2. **When?** When were the U.S. embassies in Kenya and Tanzania bombed? When did terrorists crash two airliners into the twin towers of the World Trade Center?	
3. **What?** What is cyberterrorism? What is the Department of Homeland Security?	
4. **Where?** Where did terrorists strike in Munich, Germany in 1972? Where did cult members release a deadly nerve gas in 1995?	
5. **How?** How has the United States increased aviation security? How was part of the Pentagon destroyed?	
6. **Why?** Why did the Irish Republican Army (IRA) engage in terrorist attacks? Why are some people critical of the USA PATRIOT Act?	

Guided Reading Workbook

Global Interdependence

Environmental Challenges

Key Terms and People

desertification process of land becoming desert

greenhouse effect term describing global warming, the warming of Earth's surface

conservation protection of natural resources

Before You Read

In the last lesson, you read about terrorism.

In this lesson, you will learn about challenges to the environment.

As You Read

Use a chart to take notes on factors worldwide that threaten the environment

DEVELOPMENT AND POPULATION PRESSURES
How is population growth putting pressure on the environment?

The global population is increasing at a fast rate. Population growth creates a large workforce and can help strengthen economies. It also increases the use of energy and natural resources and can create environmental problems.

To meet the needs of a growing population, industry has had to make more products faster. The burning of fossil fuels for industry has created pollution and environmental disasters and has contributed to global warming.

To grow food and build homes for the growing world population, many forests have been cut down. This leads to **desertification,** the process of land becoming desert. As a result of desertification, animals lose living space. Many animals have become extinct.

Some governments have tried to control population growth. China, for a time, penalized couples for having more than one child. India and Nigeria have tried to lower birth rates by encouraging the use of contraceptives.

People are moving from rural areas to urban areas in large numbers. This migration pattern is especially high in developing countries. Urbanization leads to increased consumption of resources such as food, energy, and water. Meeting these needs puts stress on the environment. This can affect air quality, energy resources, and the climate.

1. How is desertification linked to population growth?

_____

_____

Lesson 5, *continued*

WORLD CONCERN OVER THE ENVIRONMENT
What causes global warming?

Many people think that industrial pollution has a harmful effect on the earth's atmosphere and leads to global warming. The warming of Earth as a result of greenhouse gases building up in the atmosphere is called the **greenhouse effect.** Greenhouse gases absorb energy from the earth and keep it in the atmosphere. This makes the planet warmer. Industrialization adds to the buildup of greenhouse gases. In particular, burning fossil fuels such as coal and petroleum adds to the buildup of greenhouse gases.

Scientists think that if global warming continues, deserts will expand and cause crops to fail. Also, polar ice caps will melt, raising sea levels. Nations are trying to limit greenhouse gases from industry.

Air pollution is another serious environmental problem. Many of the most polluted cities are in Asia. Population growth in Asia causes more demand for transportation and energy resources. This increases pollution.

2. How does industrialization lead to global warming?

_____

_____

DEPLETION OF NATURAL RESOURCES; A GROWING APPETITE FOR ENERGY
How can more energy sources that do not hurt the environment be used?

Natural resources like clean water, forests, and energy supplies can run out because of industrialization and development.

Water pollution and lack of clean water are big problems in many developing countries. Eighty percent of all illnesses in developing countries are related to lack of clean water. **Conservation** means preserving resources. Using less water and using it more efficiently are examples of conservation.

Rainforests are being destroyed in Brazil and parts of Africa, Asia, and Latin America to clear land for farms and cattle. In these developing nations, governments try to protect rainforests and other natural resources. At the same time, they also want to grow their economies. International organizations work to distribute natural resources equally around the world.

Population growth has increased the demand for energy. Energy comes from renewable sources of energy, such as wind, water, and solar power. But most energy today comes from nonrenewable sources, such as oil and coal. These energy sources can damage the environment. Improved technology might create new ways to use renewable sources of energy. This would reduce pollution and global warming. Government action and regulations hope to protect the environment while also not hurting business and economies.

3. How can the use of renewable sources of energy be increased?

_____

_____

Lesson 5, *continued*

As you read about challenges to the environment, take notes to answer
the questions.

1. How are population growth, industrialization, and the environment connected?

2. How does urbanization impact the environment?

3. What do scientists say about the effects of global warming?

4. What is sustainable development, and why is it important?

5. Describe the following energy sources and give examples of each.	
a. Renewable	b. Nonrenewable

Global Interdependence

Cultures Blend in a Global Age

Key Terms and People

popular culture cultural elements—such as sports, music, movies, and clothing—that reflect a group's common background

consumerism emphasis on the buying of consumer goods

Before You Read

In the last lesson, you read about environmental challenges.

In this lesson, you will learn about the global blending of cultures.

As You Read

Use a chart to identify ways technology and the spread of Western culture affect the world.

CULTURAL EXCHANGE ACCELERATES
What has speeded up the sharing of cultures?

Changes in technology have made it possible for people to share their cultures with one another. Television is one of the main forces in this trend. It allows people to see things that happen around the world. Movies and radio have also had an impact in bringing the world's people together. But the Internet has created a sense of shared experience more than any other technology. Blogs, social networking sites, and other parts of the Internet communicate ideas and information in the blink of an eye.

As a result of these mass media, the world's popular culture now includes elements from many different cultures. **Popular culture** includes music, sports, clothing styles, food, and hobbies. American television shows have become popular around the world. Broadcasts of some sporting events can reach

millions of people in all corners of the globe. Music has also become international.

1. Name three aspects of culture that have become international.

_____

_____

WORLD CULTURE BLENDS MANY INFLUENCES
What countries have most influenced cultural blending?

Cultural blending occurs when parts of different cultures are combined. In recent times, the United States and Europe have been a major force in this blending. One reason is that Western nations dominate the mass media.

The political power of the West has also spread Western culture to other regions. For example, English is a major world language. About 500 million people speak English as their first or second language. More people speak Mandarin Chinese. But English speakers are more widely spread throughout the world. Western clothes can be seen throughout the world.

Western ideas have also influenced world thought. The Western focus on **consumerism**—the spending of a lot of money on consumer goods—has spread worldwide. Some people think Western-style consumerism is an unhealthy force in world culture.

Some ideas have also traveled from East to West. The worlds of art and literature, for example, have become more international in recent decades.

2. What Western aspects of culture have spread throughout the world?

_____

_____

FUTURE CHALLENGES AND HOPES
How has the world responded to cultural blending?

Some people think the spread of international culture is a problem. They worry that their own culture will be swallowed up by other cultures. Some countries have adopted policies that reserve television broadcast time for national programming. In other countries, television programmers take Western programs and rework them according to their own culture. In some areas, people have returned to old traditions in order to keep them alive.

The people of the world are becoming more and more dependent on each another. All through human history, people have faced challenges to their survival. In the 21st century, those challenges will be faced by people who are in increasing contact with one another. They have a great stake in living together in harmony.

3. What problems or challenges can cultural blending bring?

_____

_____

Lesson 6, *continued*

As you read, take notes to answer questions about the sharing and blending of cultures.

Cultural exchanges are taking place at a faster pace than ever before.	
1. How has technology affected the sharing and blending of cultures?	
2. Why is mass media such a powerful force in spreading popular culture throughout the world?	

Western culture has greatly influenced cultures in many parts of the world.	
3. Why does the West play such a dominant role in shaping world culture?	
4. What is one significant difference between Western cultural beliefs and many non-Western cultural ideas?	

Global interdependence has ushered in change and challenges.	
5. Why do many people view with alarm the development of a global popular culture heavily influenced by Western ways?	
6. How have different countries responded to the impact of cultural intrusion?	